San Gabriel Valley Girl
Fighting to Be Me Again

by Rosemary Beatriz Montoya

Copyright © 2020 by Rosemary Beatriz Montoya

All rights reserved. No part of this publication may be reproduced, distributed or transmitted in any form or by any means, including photocopying, recording or other electronic or mechanical methods, without the prior written permission of the publisher, except in the case of brief quotations embodied in reviews and certain other non-commercial uses permitted by copyright law.

Names of individuals and personal, identifying details have been altered to protect their privacy.

Printed in the United States of America
Print ISBN: 978-1-951490-94-2
eBook ISBN: 978-1-951490-95-9

Library of Congress Control Number: 2020922390

Publisher Information:
DartFrog Books
4697 Main Street
Manchester, VT 05255

www.DartFrogBooks.com

Join the discussion of this book on Bookclubz. Bookclubz is an online management tool for book clubs, available now for Android and iOS and via Bookclubz.com.

"I hope you never lose your sense of wonder."
- "I Hope You Dance," a song by Lee Ann Womack that my mom lovingly dubbed my fighting song.

This book is dedicated to my amazing mom, who is the main reason I am who I am today, and my wonderful Grandma Maria Betty, who has always been so loving and supportive.

My other incredible grandma will always be a guiding light.

To my dad, my four sisters, my stepdad, my stepbrother, and Max Votolato: I love you all so much.

Last but not least, I dedicate this book to my two nieces and two nephews. I never knew how much more love a family could have until you all came into our lives. You make me want to keep learning and improving myself on every level. I want to show you that anything is possible as long as you stay true to your unique heart, soul, and inner guide. No one knows you and what you want in life more than you do. Always believe in yourself, never give up, trust your intuition, follow your dreams, and remember that slow and steady really does win the race.

Prologue

We don't stay in the same place forever. Think that's a cliché? Listen: things only become clichés because of the truth that resides in their core.

I lived for years in a world where life seemed pointless—a world filled with love, horror, pain, distress, loss and torment. I'd rather have died many times than continue like that. Getting out of that place was hard. It took constant patience, love, faith, belief and courage. Sometimes there seemed to be no light at the end of the tunnel. But, once I lit a match, kept looking forward, and resolved to never give up—no matter what—time did pass. Where there once was no light, slowly but surely I started to see glimmers of hope. Time heals everything, if you let it.

This is not the start of my story, but it is a good place to begin.

I was driving. My sister Destiny was beside me. Mom had told us what freeway to get on, but instead of transferring to the 57 like we were supposed to, we got onto the 71. It was a freeway I didn't remember ever being on before. The Corona Freeway.

Confused and not knowing where we were going, I knew we needed to exit soon, but I was a new, inexperienced driver. Instead of heading for the exit, I ended up in the fast lane. We had no idea where we were, so I veered toward the escape route. The car radio was blasting "Add It Up" by the Violent Femmes.

The sun was setting. I put the blinker on, intending to get off that scary freeway—and the car just stopped! It stalled right there in the fast lane. I kept trying to restart the car, but nothing; we had gas because we'd filled the tank after leaving the house. In the middle of that busy freeway with its heavy flow of traffic, Destiny and I were freaking out.

We didn't know what to do. Back then, anyone who had a cell phone was old, or rich, or more likely both, so we couldn't call 911. I turned on the emergency lights and told Destiny that maybe we should get out of the car and run across the freeway when it looked like we could make it safely. But when would that be? Too many cars were out there, and all of them raced by. The odds didn't look good, but staying where we were wasn't an option. Plan B was to hope some nice person would stop to help us.

What actually happened was that these young guys slowed down as they drove past us, but instead of offering to help, they laughed, yelled, and pointed at us like they found the whole situation funny. How could anybody think the mess we were in was *funny*?

In those moments, we were in the universe's cosmic hands. I opened the driver's side door, stood up, and began waving my hands to make sure all the other drivers saw that we were stalled and that they should go around us. I was still hoping someone would stop to help when they saw my distress, but no one did. Nobody cared that we were stuck in the middle of a busy freeway with cars speeding by us. They saw my desperate gestures, they knew I needed help, and they ignored me.

And then it happened. An oncoming car didn't slow down and go around us like the others. It came at us at full speed, as if the driver couldn't see me standing there waving. I have the vaguest memory of my sister shouting at me to get back in the car. That's the last thing I remember.

CHAPTER 1

The Beginning

I was born at Queen of the Valley Hospital in West Covina, twenty miles east of downtown Los Angeles. I lived my first few years in Azusa, in the San Gabriel Valley, where my grandma has lived for fifty-seven years. From there, I went to Covina.

Memories are magical. A song, a movie, a TV show, a place, a scent or just a passing thought can carry us back in time. Some memories are good, and some less so. We choose which to remember. Me, I live for the good ones.

The thing about memories is that they never stop accumulating. At the end of each day, we have a bunch more that we didn't have when we got up that morning. We naturally tuck away most of our past life experiences, and before we even realize it, we're another year older and so much more of our future is on the horizon. Our past is on the back burner, but the older we get, the more precious and sacred our memories become. They may not be in our minds all of the time, but we hold on to them for dear life. We must—those memories helped mold us into who we are today. Without them we'd have no past: no mom, no dad, no friends, and no recollection of anything at all. It would be terrifying.

Of course, all of us have things we'd like to erase from our past. Things happen that no one wanted to happen. But we can learn even from those instances. Struggle and suffering can lead to the discovery that we have strength, courage, or other attributes we didn't have, or didn't realize we had, before. And then there are the things about which we can only wonder, like why we had to go through all of those hardships. In the end, we just have to take what life throws at us and make the best of it.

I was blessed to have the family I was born into. My mother, Angela, is the mother every daughter wishes for. People fell in love with her as soon as they met her. From day one, Mom was my backbone, my strength, my all. Wonder Mom, people called her. She was always making sure that everyone was taken care of. It was only when I became an adult myself that I realized how much she could have used some "her" time. Somehow, she never seemed to get that. And if you knew *her* mom, Grandma Maria, then you knew where my mom got her best qualities.

Grandpa Harry (my mom's dad) passed away when I was nine years old. All I have left of him are memories of great times we shared together. I sure did love him.

Then there were my two precious sisters, Alyssa and Destiny. It was always us three girls and my mom, and sometimes our grandma. My sisters and I have been extremely close our entire lives. We all lived under the same roof until I was about twenty-one. I love them all so much. These four women make my world spin round.

Those are my closest family members who have been there for as long as I can remember. But, there are a few more still that I haven't yet mentioned.

CHAPTER 2

My First Loves

My mom met my dad in high school. They say it was love at first sight. They dated for a while, and then Mom got pregnant, so they married. She was nineteen years old when she gave birth to me. Mom and Dad eventually had three girls: me, Alyssa, who is three years younger than me, and Destiny, who is five years younger. Mom raised us all because Dad was always in and out of jail.

I suppose I assumed then that, if you were the firstborn, everyone adored you—that's certainly how it was for me. I didn't realize it at the time because, as a child, you assume that whatever is should be, but I know now that my mom was my guardian angel.

I spent my first few years in a small apartment. Dad was in jail then, so Mom quickly became strong and independent. She had to, for my sake. But even though I didn't have a father with me all the time, I had lots of other people. I was close to my grandma and grandpa, and Mom had three brothers and a sister from Grandma's first marriage. She was the youngest and the only child to come from Grandma's second marriage, so I was never short of aunts, uncles and cousins.

Mom and Grandma read me children's books, poems, and nursery rhymes. They sang songs to me as well. I loved all of it. Those were blissful, innocent days, when it seemed that adulthood would never come calling. All I remember is being surrounded by love, for which I will always be grateful.

CHAPTER 3

Innocent Little Girl

I didn't see Dad's family as much as I did Mom's, but we always kept in contact. Mom and us girls were always close to Grandma Lucy (Dad's mom), even though he wasn't around much.

The bond between Mom and Grandma Maria was incredibly strong, and because I was her first grandchild that lived nearby, we got to be remarkably close, too. With me being so young and the only little one around, it's safe to say I was kind of spoiled. I had the world at my fingertips.

Spoiling a child too much can have negative consequences. Mom's told me all about my terrible twos, about how I threw fits all the time, throwing myself to the floor in stores, screaming bloody murder if I didn't get what I wanted. Basically, I was a little menace to society.

"I want this."

"Give me that."

It was unusual for a two-year-old to speak so clearly and to articulate demands so well, but Mom, Grandma, and Uncle Van (Grandma's second child) said that they remember me talking fluently and intelligibly at that age.

I was around two years old when my dad got out of jail. I sure did love my daddy. What little kid wouldn't love having their dad around as long as he was fun and treated them well? And that was my dad: fun, carefree, loving. And he certainly treated me well.

At the time, Mom and I were living in a small apartment in Azusa, right next door to my dad's sister, Auntie Darlene. She had two kids of her own: Michelle and Jasper. They were both a few years older than me, and they were the first cousins I ever knew. I loved living next door to them.

The only thing that separated our personal living areas was a door that connected to Michelle's bedroom. I would try to open that door so often, but it was permanently locked. My young mind considered the apartments to be all one big house. I didn't understand why I couldn't just walk through to the other side whenever I wanted. It even resembled every other door in our home.

I like reminding myself of that fearless girl I once was; those were beautiful, simple days that I'll never get back. But the Beatles had it right: "all you need is love." Having love in my life from the very beginning makes me feel like a billionaire. To think that, at one time, I never knew how important money was. I just knew we didn't have much of it. And since I didn't know anything about money, it didn't bother me that it was in short supply in our home. I was happy, healthy and energetic, content to simply be me and revel in the love that was always around. And no matter what the circumstances, my mother always made sure I was well taken care of.

CHAPTER 4

A Premature Life

One day, Mom and Dad told me I was going to be a big sister. I didn't get jealous at all. I got super excited!

We still lived at that same place in Azusa, right down the street from a liquor store that I remember going to almost every single day. I especially remember walking there a lot with Mom while she was pregnant with my sister. I always got some candy and Bazooka bubble gum. Sometimes an ice cream bar.

I couldn't wait for my new sister to be born. Then, one day, Mom was in a lot of pain and Auntie Darlene drove her to the hospital with me in the back seat. I didn't know it at the time, but she was being born way too soon. I didn't understand what was going on, except that my baby sister couldn't come home with us after Mom gave birth to her. Instead, she had to stay at that hospital in an incubator for what seemed like forever. Alyssa was born weighing one pound, thirteen ounces. Her entire head fit perfectly in the palm of Mom's hand. Mom still has that precious photograph today.

Mom took me to the hospital to visit Alyssa a lot, except I didn't really get to visit her. I was only able to look at her through a big glass window as she lay in a tiny bed. It sucked. I didn't understand why she had to be in that room, in that little bed, and why the heck I couldn't just see her close up. I would have done anything for that, or even to touch her.

And then, one day, the doctor said I could go into my baby sister's room. I was so happy. I tiptoed inside to see her up close for the first time. I couldn't believe how small she was. I'd never been around any newborn babies before, but I sure didn't think they were *that* tiny. Alyssa was such a little thing. She was also really wrinkly. She had a bunch of cords on her and a tube that went up her nose. Mom said that tube was to help her breathe. She was beautiful, and I already loved her so much. When the doctor said I could touch her, I put my finger threw a hole in the glass, and she felt amazing. I couldn't wait until the day the doctor would let us bring her home where she belonged.

Alyssa spent four whole months in that incubator before the doctor finally said she could come home. I was overjoyed. To this day, Mom raves about how wonderful that doctor was.

We had to take extra precautions with Alyssa since she was extra fragile. The love in our family only grew stronger. They say a baby brings its own love with it. They're right.

Dad was around sometimes after Alyssa was born, and I loved it. Unfortunately, it was never for long, so Mom had to navigate the hardships of being a single parent. But she still loved him, and always hoped things would change. A couple of years later, when he was home again, she got pregnant for a third time. She never thought twice about having my new sister, but after Destiny was born Mom vowed she would never have another child.

I was just as happy and thrilled with Destiny as I had been with Alyssa. Mom was, too, but she had a lot of responsibility on her shoulders. Looking back, we were poor, but it didn't seem that way to me at the time. I guess it would have made things easier if Mom had more money, but we had each other and the bare necessities, and that's really all that mattered.

CHAPTER 5

Intimidating Elementary School

My first five elementary school years were spent in Azusa, at an apartment complex for low-income families. It might have looked small to some, but it was perfect for us: three bedrooms and a bathroom with a shower upstairs, and downstairs there was a modest living room, a half bathroom, and a small kitchenette with a little space for a dining table. Outside, we had a mini patio. My sisters shared the master bedroom, and my mom and I had our own rooms right next to each other. We were happy and content there.

Mom was very involved in the PTA when I was in kindergarten and first grade. I liked that. But when she told me on my first day of first grade that she was going to walk with me to my classroom, I firmly told her no. Having your mom walk you into school was not cool.

I was very different at home than I was at school. At home, I talked nonstop and basically felt in control of things. Anytime there was some sort of gathering, whether at my or any other family member's house, I demanded attention from everyone. I loved singing and reciting nursery rhymes, and I'd tell anyone who talked while I performed to "be quiet and listen to me." But at school I was shy and quiet. I never talked unless the teacher called on me. I did everything I could to avoid attracting attention.

In fourth grade I only had one friend, and we weren't even that close. Ella lived in the same apartment complex, but we didn't talk or play together there—only at school. Sticking together at school helped us both look less like loners. I also had one enemy: Valerie. I never figured out why she disliked me so much. Maybe it was because I was so freaking skinny. I got called names as early on as I can remember: Skinny Bone Jones, Toothpick, Scarecrow, and whatever other creative names mean little bullies came up with. Or, it might have been because I didn't have the nicest clothes and shoes. I never felt deprived, but maybe deep down a little bit of that insecurity showed. I don't know for sure. Whatever the reason, she picked on me all the time, and one day, it all came to a head.

During a fifteen-minute recess, I was standing in one of the bathroom stalls when two girls came in laughing and calling out my name. Somebody was obviously looking for me. After I said something to acknowledge them, one of the girls said, "Valerie wants to fight you at lunch."

My body suddenly felt like it had gotten flushed down the toilet I was standing by. My stomach dropped completely. My nerves, my heart, my whole being was as terrified as I had ever been. I thought about telling my teacher, but that would make everyone mad at me. And in any case, if Valerie wanted to fight me, she wouldn't give up until she did. I didn't know what to do. I was scared out of my little mind.

The bell rang. Recess was over, and I had to go back to class. I left that restroom and started walking back to Ms. Sitter's classroom. Valerie saw me walking, and came right over to me and said,

"You'd better not say anything to the teacher."

Why is she doing this to me? I always stayed quiet, minded my own business, and didn't bother anyone. I wanted so badly to go home, hug my mommy, and crawl into bed.

Back in the classroom, all the other kids were staring at me. They had obviously heard what was going to happen at lunch. I desperately wanted to tell the teacher then, but knew I couldn't. Maybe I could've said that I was sick and tried to go home. Then my mom would have rescued me. My heart had never beat so fast. I decided to keep my mouth shut; it was the worst feeling in the whole entire world. I didn't know exactly what was going to happen at lunchtime, but I knew that whatever it was, I probably wasn't going to like it.

But like it or not, the time was coming. I could tell everybody around me was excited and looking forward to this "big fight," assuming I'd get my ass kicked. Valerie was not fat, but she was a much bigger girl than me, and her face just looked mean. She had a deep scar under one of her eyes. Valerie seemed highly confident, like her shit didn't stink. And mine did.

The lunch bell rang. The dreaded moment finally arrived. Everyone ran out of the classroom, while I dragged along slowly and ended up being the last one out. It didn't take long before there was a big crowd of people out in the middle of the field where Ella and I would normally sit at lunchtime. Somebody grabbed my arm and marched me over to the big event. Then everyone formed a circle around me and Valerie. Some girl started chanting, "Fight! Fight!"

As everyone huddled around us, Valerie started to bounce a little with her fists up, so I followed her lead. She threw a hard punch and a kick, but I'd always been good at dodgeball and had fast reflexes, so she missed. Every time she attempted to hit me, I got around her blows. At first, I heard voices cheering Valerie's name, but then I heard a couple of people start to cheer mine.

Then the unexpected happened; I fought back. I gave Valerie one good hard punch in her chest and she backed away as if I had actually hurt her. Then, when she came back for more, I kicked her hard with all my skinny might, right between her legs, and again in her stomach. I figured I must've really hurt her because she grabbed herself and backed away. She didn't want to fight me anymore.

I couldn't believe what was happening. Valerie looked like she was in a lot of pain. Her breath seemed shallow. Before I knew it, the fight was over. I recall girls yelling, "Rosemary won! Rosemary won!"

I was incredibly relieved—I'd won the fight, and I didn't even have a scratch on me. This was a good day after all.

What's so funny about this whole scenario is that years later, when I was in my mid-twenties, I saw Valerie at a bar in Covina called Clancy's. It had been years since our playground fight, but we remembered each other, and we finally played nicely. Months later, I got a friend request from her on Facebook. I accepted. No hard feelings. But I can't help but find it humorous, even now.

Back at home, where I was anything but quiet and always the center of attention, life was definitely less stressful for me. I would often tease my little sisters, at times being a mean and bratty older sister. And sometimes, a mean and bratty daughter. I could also be cool, fun and nice, or I could be a problem child. One could accurately say that I was another person when school wasn't in session.

My mom used to tell me a rhyme about a girl she compared me to. It was called "There Was A Little Girl." It went like this:

> *There was a little girl,*
> *and she had a little curl*
> *right in the middle of her forehead.*

When she was good
she was very, very good,
and when she was bad she was horrid.

I guess that kind of summed me up.

When my sister Alyssa was born, Mom had us both baptized together at my grandmother's church. Grandma was a proud president there and an avid choir singer. Aunt Darla (my mom's only sister) was my godmother and Uncle Allen (my mom's oldest brother) became my godfather. I had always felt extra close to them. My aunt lived nearby, and I saw her and my cousin Michael often. My uncle, his wife, and their two daughters didn't live close by, so I didn't get to see them as much as I would've liked, but he would visit my grandma and all of us from time to time.

Looking back now, I truly understand how love is the most important thing in the world. Yes, we shared an old, cheap apartment, but that was normal to me. Being tucked in at bedtime was a great ritual. Most nights I would have to sweep a thin cockroach or two off my bed or pillow before getting tucked in. They were just there. It was no big deal, but simply the life I knew. I never felt deprived at all. It seemed completely normal to live this way.

We were as healthy as could be. We always had food, water, milk, bread, and other goodies in the refrigerator. I had clean sheets to sleep on (minus the roaches), and there was a laundromat nearby that we went to often, so I always had clean clothes. Mom cooked us yummy meals. We loved going to the cheap video store down the street. We had a television, a VCR, a Nintendo, a couch, a bathroom, a shower, and all the necessities of life. We got most of our clothes, furniture and appliances at thrift stores, but what's wrong with that? We also had a car that all of us fit safely inside. I had the world's most loving, attentive and amazing mother. What more could a child want?

Mom worked two jobs, and we had food stamps to help us out. We also had a few different babysitters. One of them was Nadine, who lived in an apartment across from our patio with her mother Barbara, sister Christy, and two younger brothers Carl and Sam. Nadine always had this rugged, fun, tough side to her. She usually watched us for a few hours on certain nights of the week.

While watching us one day, Nadine came up with a game we called "The Tickle Family." She, me, or one of my sisters would get up out of the blue and yell, "Tickle Family!" Then we'd all start tickling one another until it hurt. We would go pretty far with that game, too. We'd usually only last around five minutes before the pain became too severe to handle, or basically until our stomach muscles hurt. After a Tickle Family session, I couldn't even giggle a little for the rest of the night. It hurt too much. If someone accidentally made me laugh, I'd cry out in agony, begging them to stop. I would want them to hurry up and say something sad or serious to combat the pain from my laughter. It probably sounds strange, but we enjoyed that game very much.

A place that my mom would take us to a few times a year was Olvera Street in Los Angeles. They had a long row of shops, indoors and out. It was so much fun to look at all the cool Hispanic heritage things for sale. The main reason we liked going down there was for the excellent taquitos and guacamole sauce from a small corner restaurant. I always remember that feeling of anticipation when driving up there. We all thought they were better than any taquitos we had ever tasted. It wasn't the nicest looking place, but no other restaurant could compare. We always ate our food sitting on a long bench outside the restaurant. There were three tables inside, but we never wanted to eat in there. Mom told us she'd been to a few other restaurants in that area, but they were not as good and way more expensive. The secret to that place being so good was the guacamole sauce. I would even drink that sauce if there was some leftover. It was simply to die for.

After that treat, we would stroll down Olvera Street. It always felt great being there. The shops were interesting, with the coolest stuff that I never saw anywhere else. It was fun walking around and browsing with my family. Most of the walking involved window shopping, but Mom always let us get a few little toys and some candy along the way. There were quite a few candy stands, and I loved my candy. My favorite was the strawberry flavored Tangy Taffy with sprinkles. The liquor stores that I'd go to near my house rarely had the Tangy Taffy brand. It was a delicious dessert.

Our last stop before walking back to the car was at a little fruit stand. We'd order fruit bowls with pineapple and mango, then pour as much chili powder on top as we desired. We'd eat part of it on the walk back and the other part while driving home. Those were some fun times.

The growing stages of life: I didn't know then how sacred those days were. Even the normalcy of simply getting up, going to school, coming home, eating, doing homework, playing outside with the neighborhood kids, having dinner, watching a little television, then going to bed looking forward to another day—all of that feels so distant now. They are beloved, sweet times that I know I'll never get back, but at least they live in my heart.

CHAPTER 6

Daddy Desert Days

I cherished the days spent with my dad and Grandma Lucy in the high desert. We always called it going "up the hill" when we traveled there, I guess because we were going up a hill on Interstate 15, getting closer to the mountains. Most of my memories are good, but there are a few that one might call odd.

Sadly, my dad had some demons that caused him to go to jail—sometimes for short periods, and sometimes for longer. But even when he was in prison, we still tried to keep up a relationship. Mom sometimes took us girls to visit him. He would also call us collect from jail. It was always exciting answering the phone and hearing that automated message with Daddy's voice saying, "Raymond." I always accepted the charges; Mom was cool with it. He often sent each of us letters with pictures he had drawn and colored. Daddy could draw like a Disney artist. He was brilliant.

When he was out of jail, and doing well, most of the time Dad lived by Grandma Lucy. There was only one time I remember that he had his own place and didn't live near her. How those trips up the hill worked was that mom would drive us to Hesperia to meet up with them. We would always meet at the same McDonald's, right off the freeway. They basically split the drive. It took about fifty minutes to get there, and then another forty minutes to drive to Lucerne Valley. We'd usually eat a little something and chitchat before saying goodbye to Mommy.

I was always excited to spend the weekend with my dad. He was a lot of fun, and given his circumstances, he was the best father he knew how to be. I loved him and always dreaded the possibility of him going back to jail. I tried not to think about it, but sometimes I just couldn't keep that thought out of the back of my mind. Paying child support was impossible for him, but Mom didn't hold that against him. Being a single, hardworking mother of three, she could've used the extra cash, but her main concern wasn't the money. Ultimately, all she really cared about was making sure that her kids were able to spend quality time with their father. She wanted us to know our dad. As long as he wanted to see us, she was more than willing to do whatever it took to make that happen. I'm so glad she felt that way.

On the drive up there, we'd all chat away, catching up on all sorts of things. Dad was always in the passenger seat while Grandma drove, and us girls sat in the back. He would talk a lot and make jokes. We'd all laugh. It would be a weekend of fun.

The desert is different. Everything looked so different, felt so different, and all the people seemed so different. Lucerne Valley was a quiet, desolate town. There was only one supermarket in that whole city: the Lucerne Valley Supermarket. The next closest one was another twenty-five minutes away, so, that's where we did all our grocery shopping.

There were only two places to eat out: a pizza place called Lucerne Valley Pizza, and a hamburger joint called Little Joe's, which was run by an Asian family. There was a nearby liquor store, too, but that was pretty much it. There was plenty of vacant land out there. My grandma had lots of acres at her house, and all the houses seemed to have spacious backyards too. The nearest house to ours seemed so far away that I wouldn't have even considered them neighbors.

By the time we were all settled in comfortably, it was almost time for dinner. Grandma would whip something tasty up. Most of the time we ate in since there were only two places to eat out, but at least once during our visit, we'd all go out to eat at one of those restaurants. They were okay. No matter what, though, it was fun to get out sometimes.

I loved to explore all that empty land out there. There was too much of it to see it all, but I loved to set out on my own personal missions. I'd pretend I was this explorer lost in a foreign land. I'd imagine I was all alone and didn't know a single soul. I had to explore and fend for myself. I had no food or water and would pretend I was going to have to find a new place to sleep for the night. I was a wild spirit; I loved those solo journeys.

Whenever I set out on my little journeys, Grandma told me to always bring a stick in case I ran into a coyote or something. It was a good defensive tool to have. She showed me how to use it if I was ever in danger and would tell me not to travel too far away from her home in case I ever needed to get back quickly. She would watch me as I walked out into the emptiness, and then tell me where to stop. After that, she left me alone to do my thing. That's when the journey began. And when she'd go back inside, I always went out a little further than I was supposed to.

Sometimes I ran into snakes. I saw a few coyotes, too. Anytime I saw one of those, I immediately backed away and veered toward the house. Sometimes they'd look at me, but they never bothered me. I could stay out there for hours it seemed. I recall it always being extremely hot, but it was exciting. It felt like I was on this big adventure.

Once the sun started to go down, I'd hear Grandma's voice yelling from afar, "Come back, Rosemary!" That's how I'd know my journey was coming to an end. Walking slowly back to the house, I'd continue playing that game with myself. I'd imagine I'd finally found a safe place for the night and could leave that deserted world for a while.

I can feel that little girl in me right now as I write. I feel her childish wonder. I feel all that sweet innocence that comes along with being a young girl. She makes me smile. She is me. How I miss that young girl! I loved her fearless, carefree, strong-willed ways. Her happy, creative imagination was priceless. Her precious innocence makes my entire being feel glorious even now. I feel safe. That dear child lives within me; I must let her soar more often.

My dad was an interesting man. I never knew anyone else quite like him. He was always happy to see us and tried his hardest to make sure our visits were fun and as comfortable as possible. His circumstances weren't always that good, so the visits weren't always that comfortable, but he tried. That's all that mattered.

One time, my dad took me and my sisters out late at night. I don't know why; maybe he had gotten into an argument with Grandma and wanted some space or something. He said we needed to find somewhere to sleep, and my sisters and I just went with the flow.

Nighttime in the desert isn't like nighttime in towns and cities. It's very dark, and billions of stars light up the desert sky. There always seemed to be way more stars out there. The night sky was crystal clear and everything in it so vivid. It sure was beautiful, and it gave me this out-of-this-world feeling. It was also cold—so very cold.

We drove deep into the desert that night and parked. It was freezing. I don't remember if we even had sweaters, but something tells me we didn't. At one point, we all stepped out of the car and sat on the hood for a while, looking at all those sparkling, mesmerizing stars in the sky. At that age, I wasn't familiar with the word "cosmic," but that's exactly how it felt. As me and my sisters gazed above and shivered, waiting for Dad to finish doing whatever he was doing, I thought he was trying to figure out a place we could all go to for the night.

About fifteen minutes later, he seemed to have come up with a solution. I couldn't wait to leave and blast the heat in the car. By that time, we were already off the hood, waiting for him in the back seat. That heater didn't work well, but we knew that getting on the road would be a thousand times better than sitting still in that ice cold night air.

Daddy started the car and drove away from God only knows where we were. He said we had a pit stop to make before we got to where he'd decided to go. This time, we came to an even more desolate area in the middle of nowhere. We drove up to this old broken down shack. Only the moon and stars prevented it from being pitch dark. Then, this poor, skinny dog came up to Dad. He stroked him a few times, then gave him food. He told us not to get out of the car. I felt so badly for that dog. I didn't understand what was going on. It was all so strange, like a dream. It didn't seem real, but it was. Being about ten years old, and in that state of mind, it all felt so bizarre.

He went into that shack with the dog for like ten minutes, got back in the car, and then we drove away. That poor dog. There was nothing I could do to save him. I felt sad and helpless. I'll never forget that dog or understand why he was there.

As we drove away, he started talking to us. We had no clue where the heck we were going next. I trusted my dad not to put us in harm's way, though.

I grew exhausted as he drove. It seemed like we drove for more than an hour, but I spaced out a few times so couldn't be sure. His old car made a lot of loud noises. It surely was a bumpy ride.

At one point during the drive, he told us that we were going to stay the night at one of his friends' houses. I was cold and tired, so knowing we would be stopping somewhere soon was a relief. We drove down this poorly lit block with no streetlights, or much light at all. Dad found a parking spot right in front of a house. He pointed at it and said that's where we'd be staying.

Something definitely didn't feel right. We got out of the car once more into the cold night air and started walking up to the gloomy, empty looking house. Looking at it, then at all the other houses on the block, there didn't seem to be too much of a difference between them. It might have been because it was so late at night. Still, it was a haunting scene. Dad told us to wait there as he went around back. We did as we were told.

After a few minutes passed, he came and got us, then took us around to the back of the house, where he had removed a window screen. Quietly, he said one of us needed to climb through the window and open the back door from the inside. None of this seemed normal. I knew in my heart that we were doing something terribly wrong, and I was scared.

Once we were all inside the house, Dad put the window screen back on. There was no electricity, so it was pretty dark. A side window let in the moonlight, which helped. It was almost as cold in there as it was outside. I used the bathroom even though there was no toilet paper. Thankfully I just had to pee. It was connected to a small hallway, and there was one small bedroom behind that bathroom. I peeked in, but it was all so creepy. There was no furniture inside. At least the doors and windows were locked. I couldn't help but think what we would do if someone tried to come in and hurt us.

Dad said we'd all sleep on the living room floor. It wasn't big at all, but we each found a spot on the carpet. We had no blankets or pillows, so we had to make the best of the situation. It was so cold and uncomfortable. I saw a few spiders, too, but he said it was okay. It was hard to fall asleep at first, but eventually I did.

Dad woke us up at the break of dawn, saying we needed to get going. I was still sleepy, but I got up, stretched, and used the restroom again. My sisters did the same. I was thirsty and the only water to drink came out of the kitchen faucet and tasted foul. Still, I used both my hands to drink some. We all got out of that house the same way we'd come in, and once we were outside, Dad put the screen back on the window and we left quickly.

Whose house that was, I don't know. Why we stayed there, I don't know. What city we were in, I don't know. I guess I'll never know.

We went home that day. Dad told us not to tell Mom, but in the end we did. It was hard for her to believe, but she knew he could be unpredictable at times. Mom had a talk with him later and let him know he'd better never do anything like that again!

That was by far the oddest recollection I have about my dad, but there was another time when I was around the same age that I saw a side of him I didn't understand at all. We had gone to his friend's house in Azusa. His friend's daughter, who was a little younger than me, was having a birthday party.

This was the first time I'd met any of his friends. After he parked his car, we started walking toward a house where I saw there was a lot going on. Two guys dressed similarly to how Dad was started walking toward us. These men began talking in a voice I'd never heard before.

"What up, Raymond? What's going on, *ese*?"

I thought it was weird. Then, Dad started talking just like them. He was walking differently, too; in fact, his whole personality changed. I had no idea who that guy with my dad's face was. It seemed like he was two different people. I was only ever around them all a few more times, but the same thing happened whenever he saw them.

When he was around us—my sisters, me, or any other members of the family—he spoke the way he always had. But when he saw a "homie," it was completely different. I guess in his language, a homie was a friend. I had not yet learned that term. He'd greet his homies by saying, "What up, homes?" He used the word "homeboy" a lot, too: homie, homes or homeboy. My dad sure was an interesting character.

I never understood why Grandma Lucy sometimes told my dad she hated when he went down to Azusa, but now I think she was trying to keep him out of trouble. Azusa was where all his homies lived, but he had none in the high desert.

One of the coolest things about going to Grandma's house was seeing all the different animals on her property. It was like a mini farm. She even had a pond filled with ducks. I'd hear them quacking to each other throughout the day. She had two dogs that were allowed indoors and outdoors: Boo Boo and Breaker. Her beautiful horse was so calm and sweet. I always imagined riding that horse. I asked her about it once, and she said, "That horse doesn't go on rides. He just lives there safe and sound, where no bad animals can reach him." There were also some goats and sheep. They were adorable and talked to each other in their own special language. Grandma sometimes talked about a beloved goat she'd had that was her best friend. He'd go almost everywhere with her, and would even ride shotgun in her car. "He was such an interesting and awesome character," she'd said.

I loved animals. I never had any like that at home, but I sure wished I did. Having animals around made life more fun, but the only animal we had back at mom's house was a blue and white parakeet named Little Blue. I loved my Little Blue. But, being around bigger and different types of animals was a delightful treat.

My Grandma Lucy had a boyfriend living with her for a while. He seemed like an okay man. He had two daughters, Emma and Angie, who sometimes visited when we were there. Emma was around my age and Angie was younger than the rest of us. Emma had such a calm and mild temperament, but Angie was wild. We all played and talked happily together. They had entirely different personalities than my sisters and me, but we all got along well.

Whenever they visited, Grandma would make five plates instead of three. When dinner was ready, she'd call us to come eat and we'd all come running like hungry little monsters. Having a bunch of young kids together like that naturally made us hyper and crazy sometimes. A fresh, home-cooked meal brought us together and made us sit quietly for a while.

After dinner, my sisters and I would go back to Dad's old trailer, which was behind the horse's stable. It was super tiny and uncomfortable, but we were visiting my dad and that's where he lived. We spent lots of time during the day in Grandma's house, where we also took our showers. There was another trailer right behind her; this one was bigger and much better looking, and a middle-aged man lived in it. Dad would tell us it was so much nicer on the inside, too. He wanted to live there but couldn't because that man was paying Grandma rent and that was something he couldn't do. I hardly ever saw that man. I'm not sure how Grandma knew him, besides the fact that he was her tenant. Daddy lived in the hope that one day he could take that man's place.

In the meantime, we all had to deal with staying in the mini trailer with no air conditioning. During the hot summer days there was only a little fan that was no help at all. The air it blew out was hot, but at least it was air. My dad never had much. He always roughed it out, and lived in any condition he had to. He was totally content having the bare minimum. That's how he's always been.

Holidays up there were always fun. I mostly remember celebrating Christmas and sometimes Thanksgiving, in which case we'd end up having two of each holiday because the ones spent out there were never observed on the actual day. Those occasions were spent at home.

One Christmas weekend in the desert stands out more than any other. The beautiful, classic Christmas tree was up with lots of little presents underneath it. They were never fancy or expensive gifts, but they were always practical and fun, like candles, pens, pads of paper, perfume, or little figurines. Every gift tag read: *Love, Santa*. We all knew who Santa really was. It was loads of fun unwrapping a bunch of little gifts, and it sure lasted longer than unwrapping just one or two big ones. I think Grandma knew that.

So, it was another ordinary Christmas until Grandma said that there was one more present to open. She told us to close our eyes. We happily did so, and when it was time to open them, out came running an adorable little pig. I'd never been so surprised. It was the cutest thing I'd ever seen. The little pig started licking us all, as happy as could be. It looked like he had a huge smile on his face, and I was the happiest girl ever in that moment. When we started petting and playing with him, the pig acted just like a dog. He was so much fun, and I fell in love with him instantly.

He had the sweetest, funniest and gentlest personality. He was freaking awesome! The little guy was by far my favorite present that Christmas. We even named him Christmas—for obvious reasons—and he belonged to all five of us girls. He was the best. From that day forward, visiting Dad was even more exciting.

But back at home, I felt awful whenever bacon or sausage was on my plate. I still ate it, but I felt guilty with every bite. I just didn't enjoy eating it anymore. It still tasted good, but I couldn't help but think of Christmas. How could I eat one of his kind? My pet pig had such a loving and sweet personality, and he was part of my family. I loved him. I had heard pigs were stupid, but that simply wasn't true. He was very much the opposite. Grandma had told us he was a mini pig, and therefore special. "People don't eat mini pigs," she'd said. My little mind still couldn't justify it.

Soon the guy who lived in that nicer trailer moved out, and Dad moved in. He was much happier there, and so were we. It was still small, but it had an air conditioner, more space, and it was newer.

After months of Dad living in that trailer, one day he told me and my sisters that he had a girlfriend. Her name was Anna. I was about eleven years old by this time. Anna was eighteen, and she seemed very young considering there wasn't that much of an age difference between us. She was nice, but looking at her and talking to her, I felt she was quite childish. Not a motherly type at all: simply a nice, young, inexperienced girl. And while I did feel that she was more mature than me, it was hard to take her seriously as a possible stepmom. Nevertheless, I never questioned my dad about her.

Anna and Dad became a serious couple. She wasn't a fling like I'd thought she'd be. They really seemed to hit it off. She moved into the trailer with him. Every time we'd visit, she was always there. We all liked her.

Things about our visits with Dad started to change, but not for the worse. The new trailer had a little round table, the tiniest black & white TV up high near a cupboard, a miniature kitchen that his last trailer didn't have, a tiny bathroom with a shower that was about half the size of a door, and a bedroom twice the size of that entire bathroom. A big bed fit in there, but that was basically it. It was more comfortable than the last trailer, that's for sure. We started staying there most of the time and went in Grandma's house less often. I had a feeling it was because of Bret, Grandma's boyfriend. I think he had a problem with it. He became less friendly toward us as time marched on, but at least we got to spend time with Daddy.

There was one weekend at Dad's that I'll never forget. Anna wasn't there for some reason, and I don't know where my grandma was, but I'm sure if she knew about what ended up happening that night, she would've intervened. Dad must not have wanted her to know.

I remember being so hungry, and my stomach was growling. I felt weak and I would have done just about anything for something to eat. Just a piece of bread, or a sliver of meat: anything would've made me feel better, but there was nothing. Dad knew how hungry we were, but said that he couldn't do anything about it. There wasn't any food at his place. So instead, he had us do something that he said would help take the hunger away. He claimed he'd done it plenty of times and it always worked. I couldn't understand how anything but food would make me feel better, but I heard him out.

He told us all to close our eyes and imagine a big feast with all of our favorites: chicken, turkey, salad, biscuits, gravy, and whatever else our heart desired. In my mind's eye, I saw many different foods on shiny white plates. They were all on a big cherry wood dining table with a white tablecloth underneath. As my mouth watered in anticipation, dad told us to imagine taking bites of the food, and then to savor the taste in our mouths. I got lost in the deep visualization.

I imagined biting into the yummy chicken, tasting the sweet and savory juices, eating mashed potatoes with delicious gravy. After a few minutes, I moved on to salad, biscuits and more. I tried my hardest to trick my taste buds, and I did. I relished everything that entered my mouth. After chewing and tasting, he told us to imagine swallowing the food, feeling it slowly go down our throats and settle in our stomachs. I was in a deep trance as his words guided me through the entire process. He told us to do this until we felt full. Even after his voice faded away, I continued to eat, chew, taste, savor and swallow my food. I did this for probably a good fifteen minutes until I felt satisfied. When I finished, I opened my eyes, and my stomach was no longer growling. I was still hungry, but not starving, and felt extremely tired. I was content, and fell asleep at ease. In the morning, we had breakfast at Grandma's.

That never happened again—I need to clarify that. We always had food from then on. Maybe Dad was trying to toughen us up or something. Who knows?

Looking back from who I am now compared to who I was then, I sit back and smile. I never asked many questions, even if things seemed abnormal at the time. I was simply a happy kid, full of life, wonder and adventure. Come to think of it, I didn't worry much about anything, and embraced every moment of my life for what it was. I always felt safe, taken care of, and lived every day as if it would last forever.

The very first sentence in this book reads, "We don't stay in the same place forever." I'm not the same person I was during the time I've written about, and neither are my mother and father. We are all so much better and wiser today than we were then. Most of us learn from past mistakes, and it only helps us grow stronger. My resilience, my belief that the future is a better place for all of us, comes from them and from my life experience. It's so interesting how each and every one of us grow emotionally, physically and spiritually in our own unique way. We are all just humans, trying to live life the best way we know how.

CHAPTER 7

Mommy's First Love

The times Dad was in prison were sad, and not only for his daughters, but mostly for Mom. I knew how much heartache it caused her. She was so in love with my dad, always loyal, and head over heels for him no matter what he did. She stood by his side for such a long time, but eventually she realized he just couldn't love her the same way she loved him. He had a lot of problems, but when they officially broke up, I know she was hurt and devastated. It saddened her that we didn't have our father around. She tried for us, and believed for the longest time that he'd get better one day.

Mom personified the definition of what a marriage should be. She stuck by Dad through thick and thin, richer and poorer, in sickness and in health, and so much more. She dedicated her life, her love, her spirit, her soul, her mind—her all—to my father. She would do anything for him. Why he could never even come close to feeling that same kind of love will always be a bit of a mystery to me. Yes, he had a bad heroin problem and was involved in a gang, but he had the most beautiful, amazing and incredible woman that any guy could ever dream of having. Even when he was far away in some prison cell, she waited. He just couldn't change. He couldn't help himself. He never kept up his end of the bargain.

Drug addiction is awful. It takes away one's natural spirit for life and replaces it with an almost demonic force. It takes away the very essence of one's being.

My mother didn't deserve to be in love with a man like that. It's sad, but so many of us end up learning the hard way. I guess sometimes even if your gut and intuition say it's not the smartest thing, the heart and what it wants can overpower those feelings. We can't always help who we fall in love with. Sometimes love is like a genuine precious diamond and completely real, and other times you think it is a diamond, or feel its potential for being one, but it's obvious faults point you in a different direction. Consciously and unconsciously, you ignore the signs. The heart can be deceiving. It may want. It may try to feel its truth, but at the same time, it knows it's probably not real. You continue to let yourself fall deeper and deeper in love. Then, down the road, it becomes clear that your hopes have been betrayed. You knew when you allowed them this sacred piece of your heart, when you gave your body and soul, that they might not be deserving—but you trusted them. You made yourself believe that it would work. Then one day, you had to accept that the diamond you believed in so much wasn't real; it was fake. But what doesn't kill us makes us stronger.

So many of us have someone like that in our lives at some point. I have; it was under totally different circumstances than my mom's, and only for a year of my life, but I definitely know that type of man. And to be fair, I wouldn't be here today if my mom hadn't placed her dreams in such a man.

At least my dad always wanted to stay in contact with his girls. He couldn't give my mom the love she deserved, but at least he gave us some of it. So, I guess even a fake diamond has its worth. I'm happy that I got a piece of his heart, and I know my sisters feel the same.

The times we shared together were great: gloriously fun times, sad and boring times, weird and strange times, exciting, energetic times. Whatever occurred, whatever emotions were felt and expressed, I hold it all dear in my heart. He's my dad. He tried to be there for us in the only way he knew how, and I love him.

My amazing mother made all those times possible. If she had not been made of pure love and kindness, I would not know my dad as I do today. She had every right to hate him, to be mad, angry and upset with him. But even though all those emotions surely existed, she didn't take them out on us kids. That's why I have all these precious memories to hold onto. She put our feelings and our well-being before her own. Talk about strength. A spiteful mother she is not; one could only be so blessed.

There were lots of times that Mom would go out to eat with my dad and us girls. It was cool to see them interact nicely with one another, but I always hoped my mom would one day find a love to match hers.

CHAPTER 8

Childhood Fun

Soon, Dad and Anna moved into their own little apartment in Apple Valley, which was more of a happening city compared to Lucerne Valley. It still wasn't a crowded place by any means, but there was a lot more going on there and I liked it. The apartment was small, with one bedroom, one bathroom, a kitchen and a living room. Nonetheless, it was big compared to either of the trailers my dad used to live in. The place was in between a Stater Bros Market and a little Mexican restaurant.

That apartment was comfortable, and I enjoyed my time there, but what I missed was all the animals that I could see, play with, and pet at dad's old trailer behind Grandma's house. I was sad to think we'd never see our pig Christmas again. That sucked, but ultimately, we liked the Apple Valley place much more. I'd tell myself, "One day, when I'm older, I want to have lots of my own animals."

Another memory from this time was when Dad took me, Anna, and my sisters to a Halloween party somewhere out in the desert. It was a pretty big outdoor celebration. There were other kids there, too, but mostly adults. I had no clue who hosted it or who any of the people there were. Everyone was in a costume. Dad left us alone with Anna and told us he'd be right back, so we chilled on our own and continued to scope out the party. Anna got us some soda pops and snacks to munch on while we walked around.

As we strolled through the crowd, we ran into a short, stocky, bald man dressed in a cow costume. That thing must have been customized or altered. That, or some creepy Halloween store sold it. Whatever the case, it was a really disturbing getup to look at. It looked so real, and not in a good way. The cow's nipples were depicted across his entire chest. His legs and arms were covered in the classic black and white cow design. He was standing by himself, drinking a beer.

My poor little sister Alyssa got the worst of our interaction with this pervert. We just happened to be right by him, and he leaned toward her saying, "Hey there, little girl. Want some milk?" At the same time, he grabbed and yanked on those pink, realistic looking cow nipples with a creepy, obsessed look on his face.

Alyssa burst into tears and Anna pulled us away, yelling at the cow man, "You disgusting pervert!"

She frantically searched the crowd for my dad, who had been gone for at least half an hour by then. We all wanted to leave, and I couldn't help but wonder why we were even at this party. Anna went from person to person, asking all these strangers if they knew where Raymond was. Finally, someone pointed us in the direction of a big blue porta potty. Anna banged on the door until we heard Dad's voice. Anna told him we wanted to leave, but he still didn't come out right away. He kept saying that he'd be out in a minute, but it was more like ten minutes before he reemerged.

Right before he opened the door she yelled, "We know what you're doing in there!" When he stepped out, he looked so faded. At that age, I just thought that he looked strange and unbalanced; his eyes looked abnormal for sure. I had no idea what drugs even were, but I always knew he was doing something in particular to make himself look and act like that. The difference in him was obvious, and that, coupled with his long bathroom sessions, made the signs all the more recognizable. This time, I was just glad he was with us.

Anna told him what the cow man had done. He stood there in a daze, listening to her livid voice and looking at Alyssa's tearstained face, and then at all our distraught expressions. He suddenly became furious. "Where is this guy? I'm gonna kick this guy's ass!" he shouted, storming back into the crowded party and clearly looking for a fight! I was scared, but my fear suddenly dissolved into laughter when Dad began yelling, "Where's that damn cow?"

When he finally found the cow man, Dad pushed him and shouted in his face, "You been squeezing those nipples and asking my little girl if she wants some milk?"

Anna did her best to stop Dad from hitting the guy, begging him over and over to take us all home. That creepy cow man looked really scared and tried to defend himself. Eventually, she was able to get him to calm down and walk away, and we did go home after that. I was glad Dad let that pervert have it, but once we got back to the house, the night got even more disturbing.

I remember Anna standing in the hallway outside the bathroom door, yelling at Dad again. Then he started to scream, and she pushed in the door. She started to panic, then told me and my sisters that Dad had over-dosed and she was going to take him to the emergency room. We all stayed quiet, but it felt so weird because while I knew something was wrong with him, I had no idea what it meant to overdose.

The bathroom door was open just a crack, so I peeked inside and saw my father standing at the sink, staring into the mirror. When he caught me, I didn't say a word. As he looked back at me through that mirror, the only words I remember him saying were, "I have to go to the hospital because I shot up plastic."

Of course, I couldn't comprehend that, but as I walked back into the living room to watch TV with my sisters, I knew that something was terribly wrong.

That is a night I will never forget.

Anna was nineteen when she got pregnant. When I heard the news, I was really excited. I would soon have another sister, or maybe a brother. I'd always wanted a brother. Whatever the sex of the child was, it would be cool to have another little one around.

It seemed that the longer Anna was with dad, the more she tried to act like a mother figure. She reprimanded me more and basically took charge. I still couldn't take her seriously, though. She was too young, only seven years older than me. I did find that a little odd. I mean, she was a nice girl and I would listen to her, but it felt quite ridiculous.

She always made dinner for us when we were there. They were never good. I would be so hungry I'd eat, but I can't remember ever really enjoying one of her meals. The only things she made that turned out okay were hamburgers. That was my favorite food at the time in general, so maybe I just naturally thought that was Anna's best dish. It was far from great, but still better than the burgers from Little Joe's near Grandma Lucy's house.

The most fun nights were Fridays. We'd all sit around the TV and watch the TGIF lineup. It stood for "Thank God It's Friday," and aired on ABC channel 7. It consisted of four sitcoms. The first show started at eight o'clock, right after a song that went like this:

"It's Friday night and the moon is bright. Wanna have some fun? I'll show you how it's done. TGIF!"

We would all sing along and couldn't wait for *Family Matters*, the first show, to come on. Steve Urkel was the best character. My dad loved him too. Then *Boy meets World*, *Hanging with Mr. Cooper*, and lastly *Step by Step*. All the shows ended by ten o'clock. By that time, we were all pretty tired and would soon fall asleep.

We had blankets, pillows, and sleeping bags. One of us would take the couch, and the others would spread out on the floor.

Soon, Anna gave birth to a little girl she named Haley. I had another sister. She was so cute and beautiful, with these big blue eyes. I held her and instantly fell in love. If Barbie had a baby girl, she would've looked like my new baby sister. Then, almost two years later, Anna got pregnant again. It ended up being another girl. She was just as sweet and beautiful as Haley. Anna named her Esther.

Two new baby sisters. I was happy, but I found it strange that my dad had five girls and not one boy. I remember thinking, "Maybe my dad can't make boys."

CHAPTER 9

Bad and Good

Back home in Azusa, in the busy city where I felt most comfortable, reality seemed to really set in. That's where my school was, and it's where I did my homework. Azusa is where my grandma and all of my mom's side of the family lived. That was the town I called home. Daddy's town never felt like home to me. It was more like a getaway that I liked visiting from time to time, but I would never want to live there on a permanent basis.

Mom had been single most of my life and didn't date much after separating from my dad. I do remember three men she dated while we lived at our Azusa apartment. There was this one guy who was young, hyper and carefree. They only went out a couple of times. Mom didn't get serious with another man until Marcelo came into her life.

Mom was working full-time as a waitress at a Mexican restaurant called The Lobby. It was close to our apartment, and that's where she met Marcelo. She didn't go out much, so meeting someone at work seemed ideal. Though she was still heartbroken over my dad, she let Marcelo in.

When she first started bringing him around, he seemed like an okay guy. But sometimes, it's only a matter of time until evil behaviors are exposed in certain individuals.

After she dated him for a little while, he started to come over more frequently. That turned into him sleeping over most nights. He did have his own house not too far away from ours, where he kept almost all of his things. So, even though he was over a lot, it's safe to say that he wasn't officially living with us. But it sure felt like it. We went over to his house with Mom a few times, but otherwise he always seemed to be at ours.

Slowly but surely, Marcelo's mean side started to show. The way he'd talk to my sweet mother was hard to listen to. Then, when he used that same voice on us kids, Mom would get furious. She'd tell him that how he was acting was uncalled for. I knew my mom, and she became warier around him as days went by. I didn't like it. It didn't feel right. It made me feel bad. I really started to dislike this man who had come into our lives.

He only got meaner and meaner, and then he grew possessive of my mother. I knew she was afraid of him, and I could sense mom's sadness. I could see how alone she felt. But I was just this little kid and didn't know how to help her.

There were a few times he'd hit her or push her down really hard, sending her to the floor. One time in particular sticks out in my mind. We were outside on our front porch, and he pushed her into this big bush that had lots of pointy thorns on it. Mom got scratched up and was bleeding. She started crying. Luckily, we had a friendly and attentive neighbor named Cammy, who had a two-year old daughter named Felicia. They lived alone. She was the nicest lady. Cammy was home that day and heard the commotion going on outside. She saw my mom in the bush and helped her out of it, then we all went inside her house while she consoled Mom.

Mom got badly scratched up, and that was when I decided I hated Marcelo—so did my sisters. *That piece of shit! How dare he hurt my mom like this?*

And he hurt her on so many levels. Mom checked in with us to make sure he never touched us. He hadn't, and we told her that. It was like if she found out he was hurting us, *then* she would do something major. She talked about leaving him, but was scared he might retaliate by doing something crazy. I could tell she wanted so badly to get him out of our lives, but that it wasn't going to be an easy thing to do. He knew it, too, but he wasn't going to go on his own. Many nights, I'd hear her sobbing. My sisters and I would sneak into the room and hug her. Being as young as we were, we could only do so much. She needed more; she needed someone her age to talk to.

Cammy was that lady. She was a blessing. We loved her and her daughter. Sometimes, I overheard them talking about Marcelo. Cammy seemed to be a sort of therapist for my mom. After talking with her, she always seemed to feel much better. During a trial like that, one could only hope to have such a caring friend to vent to. My mom was my angel. Now, she had an angel of her own.

I'll say it again; we don't stay in the same place forever. I could see Mom getting stronger. It wasn't drastic, but she was definitely gaining more strength. That's all that mattered. My mom's happiness and her well-being meant the world to me. Marcelo wouldn't leave her alone, though. I was scared for her. Although I never thought about death before then, scary things like that crossed my mind a few times whenever he came around. It was hard for her to go places without him just showing up. He didn't like Cammy and she knew it. It's like he could see the subtle, positive changes in Mom as well, and he didn't like it one bit.

After a while, he wasn't nice to my sisters and me, either. He did have his good days when he'd be a lot calmer. His personality often changed at the drop of a dime, though. If one of us said the wrong thing or did the wrong thing—according to him—he would snap. Most of the time he'd just yell at us, but I found him intimidating. He made me feel scared, but not nearly as much as Mom. He was way worse to her. He occasionally grabbed one of us or held us down, though it didn't happen often and it never lasted long. Then one afternoon, that changed for me.

One sunny day, while Mom was away somewhere, my sisters and I were home alone with Marcelo. I was using the downstairs restroom when I heard a loud knock on the door and Marcelo's voice screaming, "Let's go!"

I wasn't ready to go at that moment, and I told him so. When he realized I wasn't coming out anytime soon, he knocked on the door again, hard, and told me that we had to go to the store. Then he kicked the door open. I was stunned as Marcelo grabbed my hand and yanked me off the toilet; my pants were still down around my ankles. Naturally, I started crying and trying to pull my pants up. His hand never left go of my arm as he dragged me down the hallway. I was shocked, unable to believe that he was doing this to me. He was so angry as he had me hurry up and put some shoes on. My sisters were ready to go, and silently observed how he was treating me. We left the house and he proceeded to march us down to the corner liquor store. Marcelo repeatedly spanked my butt the entire way there. He kept mercilessly hitting it over and over again. We were on a busy main street called Hollenbeck, with lots of traffic passing right by us, but no one stopped to say anything. I was in a sort of daze, wondering what the hell was going on. I didn't understand any of it.

Once we arrived at the store, he finally stopped spanking me. He bought a pack of cigarettes, and then we turned around and headed home. He spanked me the entire way back. They were not just little spanks, either. He smacked my ass with all his might every single time. When we finally got home, he stopped, and he didn't say one word to me after that. He carried on like nothing had happened.

I was in so much pain I could barely walk. Every step I took was painful. My sisters and I went upstairs to their bedroom. They had a big mirror in there, and when I pulled my pants down to check out the damage, I saw what that horrible monster had done to me. Every last inch of my butt was covered in black, blue and green bruises. There wasn't a single part of my bottom that wasn't completely bruised. I began crying, then went into the upstairs bathroom to try and use the toilet again. It hurt too much; I couldn't even sit on the seat.

Mom always had so much going on, and I didn't want to add another thing to her plate. Plus, I didn't want her heart to hurt any more than it already did, so I chose not to tell her what Marcelo had done to me. My sisters and I were the only ones who knew, and they didn't think I should tell her, either. So, I kept it in.

But a week went by and I was still hurting. The more time that passed, the more gruesome my bruised butt looked. It kept getting darker, until it was close to black. Something told me that I shouldn't hold onto this secret forever. Finally, I told Mom I needed to talk to her about something. Her attention was all mine, so I came right out with it and told her everything. When I pulled my pants and underwear down to show her my butt, she immediately started crying. She hugged me so tightly, telling me how sorry she was. Mom felt so guilty, and that totally sucked. I told her it was alright, that it wasn't her fault, but she was devastated. Mom had already wanted to leave him because of his violence with her, but now that he had involved one of her kids, it was game over.

Mom talked and cried with me for a while. She kept telling me that she was going to leave Marcelo, but needed to figure out how. He was very possessive, and I got the feeling she feared for her life. I worried for her, too. It was a scary situation.

Although I felt my mother's fear, I couldn't really understand it the way I do today.

Marcelo wasn't allowed inside our house anymore. He would stop by, and Mom would tell him to leave, but he would never do so without a fight. There would always be an argument of some kind, and when he finally left, Mom would be really upset. We would all hug each other and talk for a bit.

Even though Mom obviously wasn't happy in her love life, she always seemed to recover quickly. I don't know how she did it. My mom is such a strong and admirable woman. No matter what, she was always there for her kids first. I didn't realize at that age just how amazing that was. Being a single mother with three kids, never really having a man's help, working full-time, and doing everything in her power to make sure we were all provided for is just astonishing to me now. What a mother. What a woman. What an amazing human being. We were all so lucky.

I have mostly good memories from that apartment in Azusa, days I only wish I could touch now. We made a few close friends living there. They were all around the same age as us and lived in the same apartment complex, except for Shelly, who lived in the condos next door. I always thought of the residents of those condos as our rich neighbors. They looked way nicer and the community had a pool.

We always referred to our complex as "the cheap apartments." That may have been so, but that was home sweet home, where all our good friends lived. It was all I knew, and it was all I needed.

Then, one day, Mom told us she was talking to a nice, handsome man—Sam. She seemed excited about him. I knew this guy was different. I could tell by the way her eyes lit up when she talked about him, and there was a certain special tone in her voice that I'd never heard before. It was different, a delightful different. This guy sounded special.

She went on to tell us how she met him while waitressing at The Lobby, and that they'd had an instant connection. It sounded romantic, and I hoped this guy was all that she believed him to be, but I still wanted to meet him to feel him out.

There was another interesting thing about this guy that I wasn't expecting. He had a four-year-old son named Ryan. Ryan lived with Sam, but that's all I knew about their circumstances. I didn't even think of asking why Ryan didn't live with his mother. They lived in a house in a nearby city called Covina.

Soon, Mom said that Sam and Ryan wanted to meet us. That sounded kind of serious, but cool. When the day arrived, Mom spent hours cooking and cleaning the house. She wanted us all to look as perfect as could be.

By the time evening fell, the house was spick-and-span. After Mom was done cleaning, she took a shower and started getting ready. She put on her makeup, did her hair, and put on a really pretty dress with shoes to match. Mom went all out to make herself look fabulous; she was really trying to impress Sam. There was a delicious meal cooking in the kitchen, too, and I knew we were all going to have a wonderful dinner later. Mom cooked every night, but this evening she'd obviously sprung for something more special—almost like Thanksgiving, with all the trimmings. I couldn't wait to taste it. Mom told us what to wear and made our hairstyles look super cute. Before I knew it, the doorbell rang.

Mom made sure everything was just right before she answered the door. It was all perfect. She invited them in, and there we were, all lined up and sitting on the couch. Sam and Ryan both looked really nice, and, from my young girl's perspective, handsome. We were introduced and the night felt elegant.

Before they came over, mom told me and my sisters to be on our best behavior. She was more concerned with me since I was the little rascal of the bunch. But I obeyed my mom and was as sweet as apple pie that evening. I bet Sam never even suspected there was a much worse side to me.

The entire evening went smoothly. I usually talked a lot, so it might've been a bit too much that night. I'm not sure, but that's me. There would never be an awkward, quiet moment as long as I was around. My mom and sisters said that a number of times. I sure had a big personality for a kid, and expressed it openly. We all had a pleasant time, but there was one person who didn't talk: Ryan. Beyond a quick greeting when we were first introduced, he was as quiet as a mouse—the total opposite of me. If anyone at the table asked him a question, he would just nod or shake his head. I had never met anyone so quiet in my entire life. He was sweet, and although he seemed extremely shy and nervous, he was a cutie pie.

After a few hours passed, Sam said that they should get going. It was a personable, intimate visit and we got a very good idea of one another that night; I don't think it would have gone as well if we had met at a restaurant. I think Mom was pleased by the way the night went. We said our goodbyes and then Mom walked them to their car. Once she came back in, she was desperate to know what we thought. We only told her good things.

I could feel something major was happening. I didn't know exactly what, but I really did like them. I knew Sam was a good guy, a guy that wouldn't do my mom wrong like the others. I wholeheartedly gave her my big stamp of approval and told her how interesting I thought Ryan was, and how I knew he'd talk more one day. I saw a great person in that little boy. I knew there would be a lot to learn about them, and had a strong feeling I'd one day find out.

Afterward, we watched TV together and then called it a night. I went to bed happy.

Sam and Mom only got closer. I could feel the magic between them. Summer was coming soon, and I couldn't wait. Sixth grade would start after that. Like always, I would embrace and enjoy every moment of summer when it arrived.

CHAPTER 10

Safe New Happy Life

One morning, while Mom drove us to school, she said she wanted to talk to us about something important later. That night, at home, she asked us how we felt about possibly moving in with Sam and Ryan at their house in Covina.

We were all cool with it, and Mom went on to explain how she and Sam had fallen in love and that he wanted us to live with them. It was exciting; the idea of moving into an actual house, with a back and a front yard, sounded marvelous to me.

Not long after that talk, we began packing for the big move. It all seemed to be happening so fast, and within a couple of weeks, the real work began. Mom made sure that our apartment looked great before we left. She cleaned the walls, the refrigerator, the bathrooms, the bedrooms, and everything else. Mom was always that way; regardless if the landlord was still going to charge cleaning fees, Mom felt it was still her duty to leave the apartment spotless. We also had to be very careful when packing our stuff into boxes because of all the cockroaches that lived with us. Mom told us how just a few roaches brought over to the new house could cause a major problem, so we were all on the lookout for pesky stowaways. Soon enough, everything was packed, cleaned, and ready to move to our beautiful new home in Covina.

When the big day arrived, Sam made several trips back and forth in his truck to move our dressers and beds. We all helped, but Mom carried most of the boxes while we took on the smaller ones. Moving all our things into that house was terrific, as it was much roomier than our apartment. It was a classic three-bedroom house with one bathroom, a decent sized kitchen, a dining room, a laundry room, and a big living room. As you can guess, one bathroom for four females and two males was a little rough sometimes, but we made it work.

At the new house, Ryan and Destiny shared a bedroom, I shared one with Alyssa, and Mom and Sam had the master bedroom. Sam and Ryan had a cool orange and white cat named Kitty Koo Koo. I had always adored animals, so having a new pet cat was great and it was the first cat I'd ever lived with.

I spent that summer in the nicest place I had ever lived. I can't tell you how awesome it felt to be so safe and secure. Sam and Mom were madly in love, and Ryan was learning how to share a house with three new sisters and a new mother. Though still naturally shy, he ended up coming around, just as I knew he would—we all did. Everyone seemed happy. As seconds, minutes, hours, days and then months slowly went by, the relationships between us all began to take shape. We learned more and more about one another and the feelings of love and familial bonding only became stronger.

Sam worked as a construction company foreman. He got up early and left the house by five in the morning to avoid traffic on the Los Angeles freeways. He would arrive back home in time for dinner with all of us. Mom, who had been waitressing for many years, decided she wanted a different kind of job, so she applied at a See's Candies near our house. She was hired right away, so she immediately quit being a waitress and began working part-time, then later full-time at See's. My mom is so smart and such a people person, which is probably why she was promoted to a management position within months.

I really loved the new block I lived on. I loved the name of the street, too: Shadydale Avenue. The neighborhood was full of fellow youngsters; I would eventually go to junior high and high school with quite a few of them. There were a couple of other kids that were closer in age to my sisters and brother. Destiny ended up becoming best friends with a nice girl who lived directly across the street from us. Then, to the right of her house lived a boy who was two years younger than me, and who just so happened to become my first crush. His name was Ashton.

I jocked that boy so hard! For those of you who don't know, that means that I had the biggest crush on him and wanted him so badly. I used to call him my big brown teddy bear, and I'd always flirt with him. Often, when he would have friends over, my sisters and I would be in my room and we would look at each other through our bedroom windows. We'd wave to them and dance, and basically have fun with both our windows wide open so we could watch each other play around. I even remember them putting a little stereo up to their ears one time while dancing. Then we'd start doing the same. It was so much fun.

Every night, I would stare across at his bedroom window in hopes of catching a glimpse of Ashton with his shades open, or even just seeing his shadow when they were shut. He left his window and curtains open lots of nights. When all the lights were on in his house, but his bedroom light was off, I'd sit there in my dark room and wait, knowing that eventually he would go into his room and turn that overhead on. Every time it happened, I sat and watched him for as long as he'd let me, in pure love and admiration. Many fantasies roamed through my mind. At that time, I didn't think he could possibly see me peeping on him, but now I wonder. I was so young and crazy.

Sam loved my mom so much. He once dedicated a special song to her: "Have You Ever Really Loved a Woman?" by Bryan Adams. One time, Mom was driving and that song came on the radio; that's when she told us the story behind it. I thought it was romantic, and from that moment on, every time I heard that song, I would think of them.

Later that summer, Sam proposed to Mom. She told us the great news after they'd come home from a romantic evening out, showing off her gorgeous new princess cut diamond ring with a white gold band. She was excited and looked so happy. It made me happy, too. It just felt right. Soon the happy couple hit the road to Las Vegas to tie the knot and enjoy their honeymoon.

As the summer came to an end, it was almost time for me to start sixth grade at my new school. I was excited, but also nervous. School had not been the kindest place to me in past years, but I felt more confident than I ever had before.

That year, I had the coolest teacher and I learned to play the clarinet. I really enjoyed my lessons and recitals, and my social life at school was just as intriguing as I'd hoped. I was still very skinny, but none of the kids teased me about it anymore. I wasn't as popular as some of the kids, but I fit in just fine. I was still quiet at school, but I was so much more comfortable than I used to be.

There were a few nice girls that I made friends with. A girl named Donna became my closest friend. We had an instant connection and it quickly became a long-lasting friendship. Another cool girl named Yvonne also became a good friend. All the girls at school seemed to think a boy named Gabriel was really cute; naturally I felt the same way. He even smiled at me a few times.

Soon, my sixth grade year came to an end and another sunny summer vacation—complete with slip n' slides, days spent at Raging Waters in San Dimas, water guns, water balloons, the beach, hanging out with friends, and not having to worry about homework or teachers—began. In the back of my mind, I knew I was going to be a teenager soon.

I loved my new life. Sam had rescued us from poverty and fear, and he treated us all wonderfully. Ryan became the brother I always wanted. We were lucky to have them become a part of our lives, and I know that they were just as lucky to have us in theirs, too. I adored my new life and family.

CHAPTER 11

Mean Girl

I'd made a couple of great friends on my block named Krista and Lorraine. They were sisters who'd come to Shadydale Avenue every weekend to visit their dad Peter. I was closer to Krista, probably because we were about the same age, although they were only a few years apart. There was a tomboy who lived directly across the street from them named Lanna. All the kids who lived by her seemed to get along. Lanna was okay to me whenever we crossed paths, but I always felt a negative vibe between us. I just didn't trust her.

My first day of junior high came quickly. My alarm clock went off and I swallowed my nerves as best as I could. My new school was called Traweek Middle School, which officially made me a Titan: the school's mascot. Until that morning, I didn't even know what a mascot was. Once my mom dropped me off and I said goodbye, I walked into a big part of my new life. *Here goes everything.*

I walked to the main office to get my schedule. There were so many new faces, and the school felt huge. Luckily, I saw Yvonne and Donna in the hallway, and we talked briefly. That was a big relief. Later, I had lunch with them. Sadly, we didn't have any classes together, but at least I had someone to eat lunch with. That was a good start.

I did have a class with a really nice girl named Robin. I think she needed friends, too, because she was nicer than anybody I'd met. We got along great, and she quickly became one of my best friends. I still wasn't popular, but I at least had a few good friends. Plus, not being popular gave me lots of time to concentrate on my studies. I didn't really talk to anyone else in my classes unless I had to.

Lanna, the tough girl that lived on my block, was a year older than me, but we ended up sharing a physical education class together. We barely made eye contact, but I could feel tension between us. She had this rough persona. Although we didn't talk, I still thought she was cool with me. Then one day, she started in on me in the locker room—not a physical attack, but taunts she seemed to have been saving up. For some reason, bullies exist and seem to just choose the person they want to pick on; they make them feel like shit, and these people take the heat and the humiliation that comes with it.

So, because of that mean girl, my life at Traweek Middle School wasn't as good as I'd wished it would be. But, it still wasn't as bad as it could have been since I had true friends that stood by my side.

CHAPTER 12

Living Each Day to the Fullest

One day, my friends from across the street, Krista and Lorraine, told me that their mom and stepdad were taking a vacation to Lake Mead and then to Las Vegas to see Mike Tyson fight Evander Holyfield at the MGM Grand. I knew nothing about boxing, but when Krista invited me along, I was stoked. I had never been on a fun trip like that before.

Their main house was in Newport Beach, which I'd never heard of; I only knew about Huntington, Seal and Long beaches. Her dad drove us down there the night before the trip. I couldn't believe my eyes; they lived in this beautiful white palace with so many windows that were accented in shades of white, silver and gold. From the front of the house, I could see a bunch of boats docked out back. Inside, the house was spotless. I'd never seen or been to a house so nice before. I couldn't believe they lived like this. My two friends were rich.

Krista and Lorraine showed me around their entire house, inside and out. It was a perfect one-story beauty. Their rooms were perfect, the bathrooms were perfect, the kitchen, the living room, and everything else in that house was perfect. The backyard was effectively part of the ocean, with a big deck that had water right below and lots of boats docked all around. There must have been twenty-five of them. There were no waves and no swimming going on down there, but the view was spectacular.

When Krista introduced me to her mom and stepdad, her mom came across as a nice, pretty lady. Her stepdad, not so much. He said hello to me, but was not social. The vibe I got from him was that he was, well, kind of a snob. Even my young mind sort of put two and two together; the mom was most likely with him because he had lots of money. I even remember thinking that this lady couldn't really be happy with this man. I saw the way she looked at him and I saw the way he treated her. It wasn't true love. Though, that was just my take on it. I guess he had to be somewhat okay. I mean, he was willing to take me on that cool, exciting vacation with them.

Before we settled down for bed, the sisters wanted to take me next door to show me their neighbor's house. He was an older man who lived alone, and his place was even fancier than theirs. His house was two stories, and it had a beautiful gold glass elevator in it. I had never seen anything like it in my entire life. Before we left, he let us ride the elevator up and down for fun. It was awesome.

The next morning, we awoke at sunrise. Krista took me out onto the back deck, where we all took in the most gorgeous sight I'd ever seen. The sun was barely coming up, so it was still a little dim out, but the light in the sky was so beautiful and the water looked so peaceful. The fresh ocean air smelled magnificent; it had to be the freshest air I had ever breathed in my life. I was seriously taken back by this whole way of living. I had been opened up to a whole new world of possibilities that felt more like dreams than realities.

After a long drive through the desert, we arrived at Lake Mead with two jet skis in tow. I had never been on a jet ski before, but it looked like a lot of fun. Krista started talking about how she'd teach me to use one. There was a lake house already set up for our stay, and once we settled in, Krista immediately wanted to go on a ride.

At first, she drove me around while we checked out different parts of the lake and saw lots of people out doing similar things. Some would wave, and we'd wave back. I held onto her tightly, enjoying the ride and the scenery. Lots of sunblock, lots of people and lots of laughter: everyone there was having fun, including me.

Eventually, Krista wanted to go for a ride by herself so she could show me all the different tricks she could do. I enjoyed watching her. When Lorraine and her friend came back with their jet ski, Krista told me to take it so we could ride together.

One of the different tricks Krista showed me was how she could do a 360. She made it look so easy. I was definitely a bit apprehensive about doing one myself. It looked scary, and I lacked confidence. So, we just rode around the lake together for a while.

I was having a blast until Krista started pressuring me to try and do a 360 by myself. I really didn't feel comfortable trying. She then did it in front of me one more time and verbally instructed me on exactly what to do. When she explained the secret was to hold on tight, I thought I might as well go ahead and try it. Krista told everyone around us to move out of the way because I was going to do a 360. I was nervous, but a little excited because she made it look so fun. I wanted to make a cool splash like she did.

When I was finally in position to pull off this stunt, I put my foot all the way down on the gas. Feeling the rumble of the engine, I held on tight and kept a straight course, building speed until I suddenly jerked to the side to launch into the 360. That's when I lost control completely and flew off it, soaring high into the air before landing hard on a bystander's jet ski. It hurt like hell!

I was floating in the water, but couldn't swim because the pain was too severe. A bunch of people came to my rescue. Back on land, I realized that one side of my body, from the waist all the way down to my ankle, was completely bruised. I was so embarrassed, but the pain definitely outweighed the shame at the time.

I was not yet familiar with the term "ate shit," but that's exactly what my friends said happened to me. Once everyone realized I was okay enough to not have to go to the emergency room, they started to laugh at me and crack a few jokes.

I was the center of attention at dinner that night. My "eating shit" made the stepdad laugh, and since I hadn't seen him laugh before, it was sort of cool to be the one to put a smile on his face. They told me how lucky I was that I didn't get more hurt and how glad they were that they didn't have to call an ambulance. At least I got a good story out of it.

The next day we were off to Las Vegas. I was in pain for the rest of the trip. Their mom gave me ibuprofen, which helped, and I was determined not to let that accident get me down. I was super excited to go to Las Vegas, a place I had only ever seen on TV.

Driving into Vegas was incredible. Everything was so bright and out of this world. Colorful lights were everywhere, dazzling and sparkling; it all looked like so much fun. Once we got out of the car, it was even better. All the lights, all the people, all the loud noises and laughter around me: it was so lively, and the most upbeat place I'd ever been to. There was so much going on that I forgot about my pain. I was ready to have a great time.

When we checked in at the MGM Grand, us girls all shared a room with two beds, and the adults had a room that connected to ours. They were going to the big fight soon, so we were given some money and got to do basically whatever we wanted. We walked around a few of the casinos, but mainly stayed at the one in our hotel. We browsed the indoor and outdoor shops, ate a few snacks, had some non-alcoholic drinks, and just enjoyed ourselves.

Later, I noticed a big crowd forming outside our hotel lobby. I wanted to go check it out, but no one would go with me. I told them I'd be right back and ran over there all by myself. There were so many people, but I was little enough to wiggle my way to the front, where there was a red carpet. As I looked up at all the adult faces around me, they looked so eager and excited. Soon, I heard several of them yell, "He's coming!"

I asked a man standing beside me who was coming, and he said that it was Mike Tyson. I didn't know who that was at the time, but I figured he must have been a pretty big deal if the crowd's excitement was anything to go off of. No one seemed to care or even realize that I was there. There was so much commotion going on around me and I was just having fun being in the middle of it.

Then I saw this big guy walking down the red carpet. Everyone seemed so enthusiastic and put their hands out in the hopes of touching him. Being the little follower I was, I did the same. As the man got closer, he made eye contact with me and gave me a little shake of the hand. I was so happy, even though all I knew was that he was very important. After he gave me that shake, I made my way back through the crowd to where it was calmer. I couldn't find my friends, but eventually they found me. Krista was worried, asking where I'd been, so I told her everything.

The next morning at breakfast, she told her folks about what I had done. Her stepdad asked what color clothes the man was wearing. When I told him, he said it was Mike Tyson's hand I shook. I already knew this because the man in the crowd had told me. But I didn't tell him that. I just smiled.

CHAPTER 13

High School

I finally started high school. Within a week, I ran into Lanna, the mean tomboy who harassed me in junior high. She started right in again with the same insults, but even if she hadn't changed, those around her had. They'd grown older and were too mature to give her comments any attention. I could see she wasn't as confident as she once seemed. She couldn't harm me here. A big weight was lifted from my shoulders with this realization.

One thing hadn't changed, though. It seemed like all the girls at school had developed a body—except me. I worried that maybe I never would, but there was nothing I could do about it.

I wasn't one of the in-girls or Miss Popularity, but I had good friends, and I was doing well in my studies. I loved learning, and I was a great reader. So, anytime a teacher would ask if a student wanted to read aloud, my hand would always be one of the first in the air. English was my favorite subject. I wanted to know everything there was to know about the English language.

I was still shy my freshman year. I kept to myself in all my classes, and the only real interactions I had with other people were with my friends during break and lunch. I had three best friends: Robin,

Donna and Yvonne. Soon, there was another girl who started to hang out with us and became a good friend: Malerie. We shared our deepest secrets and trusted each other to keep them.

One day, as I was walking to class, a junior student stopped to talk to me in the hallway. I had never spoken to this guy before, but I had seen him around. I never even really talked to guys unless I was assigned to partner with one in a classroom. Out of the blue he said, "Don't worry, by senior year all the guys are gonna jock you."

I gave him a sweet, shy smile and a soft thank you, then we went our opposite ways. That was the first guy who had ever shown me that sort of attention. I was all smiles for the rest of the day; it really is quite amazing how much one sincere compliment can lift your spirits.

Ever since I was a little girl, I remember being told, "Sticks and stones may break your bones, but words can never hurt you." Even at a very young age, I knew that old saying was bullshit. My mom used it sometimes to try to make me feel better, but in my heart of hearts I never believed it. Even though it usually came from adults, I just knew it wasn't true because words *could* hurt me, that meant that whoever made up that saying was wrong.

Antonio was a cute boy I had a huge crush on. He wasn't popular or full of himself, so he would actually talk to me. We had moments where we would sort of flirt with one another. I had never kissed a boy, but it felt like everyone around me had, so I was anxious to kiss a boy, too. I daydreamed about kissing Antonio.

The Sadie Hawkins dance was coming up. It was a unique dance where the girl asks the guy out, instead of the other way around. Naturally, I had the perfect boy in mind. I just had to gather up the courage. My first kiss *had* to be with Antonio. That was my mission.

The day came when I was finally bold enough to ask him to the dance. I think what pushed me over the edge was that my friend

Robin overheard a girl named Kathy in one of her classes telling her friends that she planned to ask him. That told me it was now or never.

When the class I shared with Antonio came around, I asked him, without any kind of hesitation, if he would go to the Sadie Hawkins dance with me. I was so nervous, but also curious as to what he would say. Right away, he said yes. I couldn't believe it! I was beyond happy. And then word got around that Kathy had asked him but he turned her down because he was already going with me, and that just put the icing on the cake.

Tradition said couples at the dance had to wear the same shirt as each other, so Antonio told me to just pick the shirts out for us and he would pay me back once I bought them. Since my friends were going to the dance too, we decided to hit up the mall together. I chose these cute white shirts with Donald Duck on them, and a black rim around the neckline. I was thrilled; this was going to be the most fun night ever.

By the time I got dropped off at the school, Antonio was waiting for me. He looked so cute wearing the shirt I picked out for us. There was still one potential problem, though. I had no clue whatsoever how to slow dance. At first that didn't matter because the songs were fast and I could sort of move to the tune. But when a slow song started playing, I was in trouble. I didn't know how to move to the rhythm without stepping on his feet. We finished the song, but I was mortified the entire time. After enduring that long-ass slow dance, Anthony pulled my hand and said, "Let's go outside."

Was I going to get the kiss I longed for, or were we just going for a nice walk? I just relaxed and went with the flow. He held my hand and we walked through the school like that: hand in hand. I never wanted the night to end.

We stopped in a secluded area by the principal's office. With no one else in sight, he leaned over and kissed me. It was a French kiss, and since this was my very first kiss, I don't think I was very good at it. But then, neither was he. Regardless, I remember it feeling like heaven on earth kissing this guy I had such a big crush on. Our tongues locked for about thirty seconds. We sort of wiped our mouths after and then slowly walked back to the gym. We never danced again. We just had a drink together and hung out until the dance was over. Afterward, his mother drove me home and, just like that, my fantasy dream night was over.

My freshman year turned out to be far more exciting than I'd anticipated. I'd had my best buddies by my side, no problems with Lanna, easy classes, and all in all a pretty low-key, fun year.

CHAPTER 14

Coming Out of My Shell, Pot First!

The most incredible thing had happened to me over summer break, before the start of sophomore year. I gained a decent amount of weight in all the right places. Talk about coming back to school in style. I went up two bra cup sizes, from an A to a C, and even my butt had rounded out. It was all very thrilling, and I was extra excited to begin my tenth grade year. I looked better, I felt better, and my clothes fit way better. My mom even let me dye my hair with blond streaks, and I decided to start wearing a little bit of makeup. Naturally, my confidence and self-esteem were greatly improved.

When I met up with my school friends, I felt like my shyness had melted away. I became much more talkative, like the way I was at home. I started cracking jokes in class and found out I was funny. I felt more relaxed, and, for the first time, I even got in trouble for talking too much. I had become an extrovert and I was blooming on all different levels. I guess I became a bit more of an open book.

There were good parts to being the new me at school, but all these changes started showing in my grades, too. They were no longer just As and a few Bs. Some were replaced with Cs. I even remember getting a C-, which made my mom sad. I didn't seem to mind it much, though.

The new me also started attracting different kinds of people that never noticed me before. This rang true with both boys and girls. For the first time, I started to hear about how certain guys thought I was cute. Not the most popular guys in school, but part of the in-crowd nonetheless. This was also when new female relationships started to emerge. My best buddies were all great, but they were pretty much known as "good girls." We weren't nearly as good and preppy as some of the other girls, but I have to say, we weren't really popular, either. Popularity was something I'd always wanted, and the new girls I ended up hanging out with were much more popular.

I started talking to a girl named Dakota, who was a big flirt with all the guys and who walked with her head held high and her chest and butt sticking out. We had a class together and got along great. Then she introduced me to her cousin Gizelle, and I got along with her even better. Lastly, there was Stacey, a girl I had admired since junior high. I had a class with her back then, but she'd never even looked at me twice, so she didn't know who I was then. She was very outgoing, and I was still very shy. Sometimes I would just look at her and admire her beauty and the fashionable clothes she wore. I ended up having my favorite class with her—English—and it turned out that she loved reading aloud just as much as I did. She sat right in front of me and we soon became friends.

One day after class, she asked me if I smoked weed. I told her how I tried it once and really liked it, but that was basically it. She invited me to join her and her boyfriend Ricky, who happened to be one of the most popular and cutest boys in the whole school, to "blaze it" after school.

From that day on, Stacey and I became inseparable. It was always either just me and Stacey, or all three of us hanging out. Just about every time Ricky would pick her up, I was invited to join. I started looking forward to blazing some Chronic or Kush after school every day. Ricky had Orange Kush a lot, and it would get us so high. Then, we'd drive around town, smoking in his black Acura Integra.

It would be easy enough now to look back at that time and blame myself, but I'm not going to do that. I had some of the best times of my life smoking with my friends. Yes, it did come with consequences—my grades dropped, I started not to care as much about certain things in my life, and I became interested in trying other stuff—but that's just who teenage Rosemary was. We have to accept that we were who we were then, and that the decisions we made felt right at the time. Living in regret is torture to the soul, and doesn't change a damn thing. Would I advise another teen to throw herself into the drug and party scene as enthusiastically as I did? No. If I could go back in time, would I advise my young self to choose a different route through life? No, I wouldn't. For better or worse, that was me.

As my new friendships grew, my old friendships began to fall to the wayside. I hadn't cut them off completely, but they could all see the drastic change in me. It's sad, but I really enjoyed my new friendships, especially with Stacey. Donna was the only one in my old clique that had branched out, too. Not to the extreme that I had, but she got along and hung out with my two new friends Dakota and Gizelle. None of them hung out with me and Stacey, though. We were our own little set. I allowed it to happen. Stacey was my stoner friend, and Dakota and Gizelle were my party friends.

When Ricky would pick Stacey and me up from school, there would be a bowl of weed waiting for us to hit. Often, we would drive around, looking at beautiful scenery, then sometimes we'd grab a bite to eat. Other times, we would go to one of Ricky's friend's houses to blaze it some more. There were usually a few "heads" there, and we'd get really high. We'd hang out at Ricky's house sometimes and just chill, all stoned. I'd go to Stacey's house a lot as well. She had a big room with tons of stuff in it, so it was never boring. There was lots of chilling, talking, laughing, listening to the radio, blazing it, and blowing the smoke out of her bedroom window.

She also had the biggest closet I'd ever seen and it was full of clothes and shoes. I envied her a little. While she talked to her boyfriend on the phone, I would snoop around and look through all her things. She knew what I was doing, but didn't care. She trusted me, and for good reason; I would never even think of stealing from her. Plus, if I really liked something of hers, all I had to do was ask and she'd let me borrow it. We borrowed clothes from each other a lot, she just had more things that I wanted to borrow than the other way around. The clothes she had in her closet, so many beautiful hair barrettes and other things: I used to think she had everything. Every time I was there, it felt like I was in a princess's room.

We had a lot in common and got along wonderfully. She was crazy at times, not to mention a risk-taker. I had never met anyone like her before. Oftentimes, I just went along for the ride. Her way of living was so carefree, and she never worried about anything bad ever happening to her. For example, she fearlessly hitched rides all the time, and because I was usually with her, I would be right by her side, doing it, too.

We once hitched a ride with a bunch of *cholos* in a nice low rider. When they stopped to pick us up, they happened to be smoking a fat blunt. The first thing Stacey said when we got into their car was, "We hitched a ride with the right people."

The *cholos* were really nice, and after smoking us out they dropped us off at Stacey's house. I didn't realize how lucky we were back then though, I just thought that was the way people were: harmless, nice, and willing to give us a lift to wherever we needed to go. We took the bus a lot, but hitching always got us to our destinations so much faster. I soon started taking risks like she did and, like her, I didn't even think twice about it.

Another quality of Stacey's that I liked was how vocal she was. Nothing ever stopped her from speaking her mind. I thought I talked a lot, but she never hesitated to say or do anything. This often led to unnecessary confrontations, and other times her uninhibited actions involved stealing whatever she wanted from certain stores. She would put makeup, jewelry, food, or whatever she pleased into her purse, as if she was just entitled to it. I had never stolen anything, but would watch in amazement as she got away with it. Nothing bad ever happened to her, either. She never carried a small purse, only big ones, so I figured that's how she had so much stuff in her room.

Our relationship only grew stronger as we hung out more and more. Stacey was so unlike my other friends. I guess I found her attitude and mischievous, rebellious ways appealing. Even though I was obviously not like her, I really looked up to her, and soon started following in her footsteps in a lot of ways. I also thought she was the most beautiful girl ever. People sometimes compared her to Angelina Jolie, or Mila Kunis from the popular TV show *That 70's Show*. She was an only child who lived with her mom and stepdad. At home, she had rules and curfews, but for some reason she acted like they didn't apply in the outside world. I don't think her mom even knew half the stuff she was doing when she wasn't at home.

Once, I stayed over her house on a school night; we planned on catching the bus for school the next day. That morning, she took me into her kitchen and said, "Let's take a shot of whiskey." Her parents loved whiskey, so there was lots of it around, but I had never drank alcohol at her house. Besides, I thought that a shot right before school, before I even had breakfast, would be gross. We'd already taken a hit of weed, but that was a given; a shot of whiskey now, too? *Scanless!*

My sisters and I always said that instead of the actual word "scandalous." It was just our thing.

Stacey poured us both a shot. She just took hers and waited for me to do the same. Then I took it. Horrible! We went back into her room to smoke one more hit of weed to try and get rid of the nasty aftertaste. I felt really faded and couldn't believe we had to go to school. I was really worried a teacher would notice. We always used Visine after smoking to cover up the red in our eyes, and I knew this would help a little, but still, I was scared.

At school, nobody seemed to notice anything different about me. It was pretty hard to concentrate in my first few classes, though. After a few hours the high wore off and I just felt tired. During break I bought a few snacks from the student store. Then, when lunchtime came around, Stacey and I smoked another hit of weed and ate at Jack in the Box. I ate there on so many of my lunch breaks since it was my favorite: two tacos, lots of hot sauce, a medium order of curly fries, and a medium lemonade. Sometimes I would get a chicken sandwich, jalapeño poppers, or chicken strips, plus lots of barbeque sauce and ranch dressing.

My other friends—Dakota, Gizelle and Donna—never really talked to Stacey, and if they did, it was only briefly when we happened to be together. Dakota was a cool friend, but known around the school as somewhat of a slut. She was by far the biggest flirt in the whole school. I never understood how she could be like that. I flirted with guys sometimes, too, but Dakota took it to a whole other level. When it was just us, though, she was really cool. I liked her, but Stacey did not approve of our friendship. So, my relationships with both girls were kept separate. Basically, if I wasn't with one, I was with the other. Then there was Gizelle, we had our own special friendship that didn't include anyone else, but she didn't really like smoking weed. Donna and I always stayed friends, but as time went by it seemed like I'd hang out more with the other girls. Robin, Yvonne and Malerie, my longtime loyal friends, soon became more like acquaintances.

I started going to lots of different parties and meeting people from other high schools. Drinking at parties was cool, but I always preferred weed to alcohol. When I did drink, I always needed to balance it out with weed in order to feel whole. There were times when I didn't feel like drinking, but if I had a smoke then I was in for a good time.

I pretty much always had some weed on me, but if I didn't then there was always someone who did. I never heard of anyone having marijuana licenses back then; I'd always just assumed you had to buy it from someone who knew someone who grew it. There were always a few people at school who sold it, or knew someone who did, and there were only a few occasions during high school when the local weed supply ran dry. All the smokers hated those dry periods. We would scrape the resin out of our pipes so we could still get high in the meantime. It wasn't nearly as good, but it was better than nothing. Finally, when word got out that someone had some weed to sell, the stoners would be happy again.

Getting high and eating at Jack in the Box in Covina was a ritual I loved performing with my friends. If I wasn't with Stacey, then I'd go with Dakota, Gizelle or Donna. All of us girls became very friendly with Leroy, the restaurant manager. He was very cool and sometimes he would hook us up with discounts.

One day, I heard Leroy had hired Donna's younger sister Tiffany to work there. She was only fifteen, and since we were all sixteen and eligible to start working, we wanted to work there, too. Soon, the Jack in the Box right down the street from my high school became my very first job.

I worked part-time after school and on weekends. Sometimes I'd work up front as a cashier, and other times I'd be the drive-thru window girl, taking orders over the intercom and serving drivers. It was so much fun working there and even more fun whenever I got to work with one of my friends. I was making money for the first time in my life and it felt great. On my breaks, I would always order something off the Jack menu and take advantage of the twenty percent employee discount.

I almost always went to work stoned. At the time, I had been smoking so much weed that I never got too high to function properly. Being stoned felt normal, so it didn't interfere with my daily activities. If anything, I felt like weed improved my overall abilities. I guess you could have called me a highly functional stoner.

During this period in my life, I split my time between hanging out with Stacey and Ricky, and keeping up my friendship with Dakota. But juggling the two was hard. I knew Dakota wanted to hang out with us, and I felt the need to get all three of us girls together. Although Stacey wasn't thrilled with the idea, she did eventually agree to give it a shot since Dakota was a friend of mine, which meant there must have been something good about her. Stacey also liked the fact that she blazed it, too.

The first time we all got together was at Stacey's house. She invited us over after school to hang out and blaze it in her princess room. We ended up having a great time talking, laughing, and listening to the radio together. We were all stoned when a Bob Marley song that none of us had ever heard before came on the radio: "Three Little Birds." Once that song came on, we immediately fell in love with it, and since there were three of us there in that stoned, creative mindset, we decided that song was a sign that our friendship was meant to be. Stacey, being the more outspoken one of the bunch, brought it up first and said that the song had convinced her that Dakota was worthy of our friendship.

A couple of days later, when Stacey and I were alone, she told me she found Dakota cooler than she'd expected and I was soon able to combine my separate friendships into one. I thought this was the start of something good.

Soon, Dakota started coming along for rides with me, Stacey and Ricky. That lasted only a short while, until Stacey confided that she felt Dakota was too much of a flirt around her boyfriend. I tried to explain that it was just her nature, but Stacey didn't like it and she told me that she didn't want to hang out with her anymore. It made me feel a little weird, and knowing I had to tell Dakota what Stacey said made me feel even weirder.

After I told her, Dakota became upset with Stacey. This left me with two friendships again, and juggling them was even harder than before. While Stacey and I continued to hang out often, Dakota and I saw each other less and less. I could tell Dakota was jealous of our closeness.

Later, Dakota started to hang out with this girl named Sandra, a Samoan party girl from South Hills, which was a nearby high school. I remember they met at a kick back that we went to one night. I guess they hit it off, and once their friendship became more involved, Dakota and I stopped talking completely.

I still talked to Gizelle and Donna, but my old friends had become distant. They weren't happy that their once best friend was spiraling down a bad path. Seeing the big changes in me, realizing how much weed I was smoking, and knowing the kind of parties I was going to and how far my grades had dropped made them feel like they had to do something to let me know how they felt. They wanted to have an intervention, but I didn't let that happen.

As close of friends as Stacey and I were, she had another friendship with a very nice hippie girl named Misty. When she introduced me to Misty, I knew she had one thing in common with us, and that was a love of smoking weed. They also both shared a dislike of Dakota.

When I started to hang out with them, Misty would talk about what a slut Dakota was, about how she was always flirting and trying to hook up with her boyfriend. Dakota and I weren't talking at this point, so I had nothing to really say. I would just listen.

I still saw her around sometimes, but we ignored each other. When we were still friends, she'd mentioned a number of times how much she didn't like Misty. I didn't know why and I didn't ask. But once I started hanging out with Misty, I understood the problem and that Dakota was to blame. I had seen her interact with Misty's boyfriend a while back, and he wasn't innocent, either; when she flirted with him, he flirted right back. Dakota had told me so many stories about different guys. I would always listen, and I never judged her. I don't know why. I knew some of the stuff she told me wasn't right or cool, but I just accepted that this was who my friend was. Some of the stories she told me blew my mind. There was always some guy she was interested in. She would literally tell me about every single guy she'd been with—whether he was in a relationship or not—and every guy she wanted to be with—again, whether he was in a relationship or not.

One hot and sunny day, Stacey, Misty and I went to the Venice Beach boardwalk. I had been there a few times before and knew it was the perfect place for stoners because you could pull out your pipe and smoke in public. Nobody seemed to care, and it was dope to be able to smoke so freely in a public space like that. There was lots of laughter, shopping, drinking ice cold drinks, watching funny street performer acts, and just having a fun time that day.

CHAPTER 15

Unfaithful

It was the summer of 1999. My teenage life was rebellious, sweet, and sometimes naughty. I always lived each moment to the fullest. Kind of like a cat. I didn't think much of the past, or the future; I just breathed and embraced life for what it was. The way I saw things through my teenage eyes was a bit strange, to say the least.

While I was working at Jack in the Box, I befriended a coworker named Jessica. Soon, she introduced me to her best friend, Bella. They were both nice girls, but what made them different was that they did a drug called speed, or methamphetamine. One day, we were hanging out and they offered me some. I tried it. We had a fun day, but the crash was horrific.

One weekend, I went to a house party with them. I invited Stacey, but she couldn't go for some reason. I got so faded that night. I drank. I smoked. I even did meth. When I got dropped off at home around one o'clock that morning, I was feeling wired from the meth. I didn't have any pot, and I couldn't fall asleep for shit. I desperately needed weed to help calm my mind down. I knew exactly who would have some, and would surely be awake: Ricky.

I paged him using pager codes to ask if he had any weed. He

did, and before I knew it, he was knocking on my bedroom window. I had to twist the handle around and around again to open it. It didn't have a screen, so he easily climbed inside.

Sam had built on additions to our home, which included a master bedroom for my mom and him behind the living room, so I didn't have to worry about them hearing anything. Everyone was sound asleep. Once Ricky was inside my room, we talked briefly, then he packed a bowl for the two of us to smoke; he had brought his bong in a case. As he packed the bowl, I started telling him about my night, and how messed up I was. I didn't tell him I was tweaking, though.

Ricky had this sexual look in his eyes as he handed me the bong to take greens, or the first hit. I blew the smoke out of my open window and coughed, then he took his hit. By then, I had an intense high going on. When we were down to the last hit, he shotgunned it to me. We both coughed a bit, then started kissing. I felt higher than a kite with all of the drugs in my system. The kiss lasted about sixty seconds before I started to pull away.

He looked at me and smiled. Just then, we both realized what we had done. It was like we couldn't believe we actually went there. My stomach dropped as he immediately started packing another bowl. This time it was a one-hitter for each of us. After that, he gave me a hug goodbye and hopped out of my window. I watched him get into his car and drive away. Just like that, he was gone with the wind and nothing would ever be the same again.

The next day, I felt horrible. I had betrayed my best friend, and coming down off all those drugs made everything worse. The damage was done. I couldn't take it back. I screwed up royally. I felt weird around her, like I'd crossed an unforgivable line. I could never truly be the same Rosemary she loved, and Stacey could never be the same to me. I knew I couldn't keep this a secret forever because the guilt would be too overwhelming. My actions had ruined our friendship, and she didn't even know it yet.

One day, I told my tweaker friends what I had done. I needed to tell somebody. I didn't want to hurt Stacey, but cosmically I already had.

One of the girls ended up telling Dakota. Even though we weren't talking anymore, Jessica and Bella were. I knew it would be too hard for me to tell Stacey to her face; deep down, I think I wanted to get caught.

One afternoon, while I was home alone, the telephone rang. It was Dakota. I was surprised to hear from her, but she was being super nice. I thought that maybe she was trying to rekindle our friendship. It was nice to hear that familiar voice.

A few minutes into our conversation, she asked me if what she'd heard about me and Ricky was true. I knew where she got the information. I felt safe confirming the rumor. I knew so many dark secrets about Dakota that I really didn't think anything of it. Her dirty little secrets had always been kept in the volt of my heart, so I just assumed she would do the same for mine. We only talked for a few minutes longer. Once we hung up, I felt an ugly feeling in the pit of my stomach.

My stepdad always liked leaving our front door unlocked during the day, even when he wasn't home. So, nobody ever thought twice about locking it. After I got out of the shower, a white towel wrapped around my body, I heard the front door slam open and hit the wall. Then, I heard Stacey yelling, "Rosemary! Rosemary!"

Startled, and with no time to think or react; I walked slowly into the dining room, which was connected to the living room. As I rounded the table, Stacey pushed me to the floor. My towel slipped off and she started beating on me. She punched me over and over again, on my face, arms and chest.

She sat on top of me for about five minutes, hitting me and screaming at me. Lying on that hard wood floor, I got my ass beat while Stacey shouted, "How could you do this to me you little bitch?" I looked across the living room and saw good old Dakota and her South Hills friend, Sandra. I couldn't believe they were just watching like that; it felt awful. It was like they enjoyed seeing me get my ass kicked.

Finally, there was this little break. She stopped hitting me, but kept yelling at me! At that point, her hold on me wasn't as secure, so I had room to move. Out of pure reflex, I was able to get myself up and run away. As soon as I entered my bedroom, I grabbed the phone off my bedside table, dialed 911, and threw it on the bed. I knew the police would track down my house for just the call. It all happened so fast.

When Stacey came in behind me, I grabbed my table lamp as a weapon. I was standing on my bed completely naked while she kept screaming at me. She tried to get to me a few times, but I warned her that if she touched me again, I'd smash the lamp over her head. For every attempt she made, I showed her that I was more than willing to hit her over the head with it. I must have scared her, because she eventually backed off. I was in control now and kept her at bay.

Dakota and Sandra were standing in the doorway, watching the entire show. I looked at Dakota again in pure desperation. I know she could read my eyes that I was begging her for help. Stacey told me she'd heard everything while I was talking to Dakota on the phone; it was a three-way call. I'd told Dakota I was home alone, and she had been over to my house enough times to know that my front door was always unlocked. She totally set me up.

I knew she was jealous of our friendship, but didn't know she wanted something like this to happen. I can't tell you how many girls' boyfriends she actually had sex with, but I never said a word. It was hard to believe that this was happening.

Although I was hurt by Dakota's actions, I knew that I was ultimately to blame. I'd betrayed my friend and I was getting paid back for it. Meanwhile, I kept standing there, nude on my bed, wondering if the police would ever arrive.

Suddenly, I heard Dakota and Sandra yell, "The cops are here! The cops are here!" They left Stacey behind.

She looked me dead in the eyes and said, "You know you deserved this, Rosemary." She walked away, and I hurried up and put some clothes on before I went outside.

There were two police cars and three cops standing in my driveway; the other girls were already talking to them. I walked right up to the officer that Stacey was speaking with. He asked me what happened, and I told him the whole story. When he asked me if I wanted to press charges, Stacey looked at me, and her eyes reflected the same thing she had said earlier. "*You know you deserved this, Rosemary.*" Feeling shaken up, I told the officer that I didn't want to press any charges.

The policeman then told the girls to go home and not come back. As they drove away in Sandra's car, he told me that if I ended up changing my mind later, I could just go down to the police station. I thanked him, but I had no intention of pursuing this any further.

Still stunned, I walked into my house, closed the door, locked it, and sat down on my couch to process everything. At some point, I went to look in the mirror to see the damage that had been done and cleaned myself up. I knew in my heart that I deserved this. Two friendships of mine were definitely over.

CHAPTER 16

Change of Scenery

When it was time to go back to school, things were definitely not the same. I knew that everything I was doing was trouble and I wanted to get away from it all, so I convinced Mom that I should go to the local continuation school: Fair Valley. Since my grades dropped after I became "that kind of girl," I felt I'd be the perfect candidate. I saw attending this new school as a sort of "get out of jail free card."

Once I started attending Fair Valley High, I'll admit that it felt so much chiller because popularity wasn't the main focus among the other students. Fair Valley was a school for failing students who had taken the wrong path. I was grateful to be there, and I made the best of it.

Meanwhile, my home life wasn't so great. I was out of control, rebellious, and so self-absorbed that I didn't listen to my mom anymore. Instead, I was ruthless, defiant, and constantly talking back. I would go out wherever and whenever I wanted, and I didn't obey my curfew. There was one night I remember going out and didn't come home until the next morning. Mom thought something horrible had happened to me, that I might be dead. I didn't understand what I was putting her and Sam through. I wasn't always nice to my sisters and brother, either.

Sometimes what you need is a break and a change of scenery. Things became so difficult for Mom, and she was so worried about my reckless behavior and well-being that after having a talk with Grandma Maria, she told me they had decided it would be best for me to go live with her for a while. She lived alone in a three-bedroom house in Azusa, which was only a city away, so it seemed like the ideal solution.

When I moved in, I took the bedroom furthest from hers so she couldn't listen to everything I did. I loved it. Since I was still working at Jack in the Box, I got transferred to the Azusa location. Everything was working out smoothly. My grandmother and I became even closer than we already were. I loved being the only kid in the house, and over time I became much more compliant. I'd still see my family, but we all got some space, too.

Having my own room again felt like having my own personal sanctuary. My grandma was very laid-back and easygoing. She wasn't strict, but she still had her rules and I obeyed them. I will admit that when I wasn't at school, doing homework, working, or just kicking back at the house, I still went out and partied sometimes. Gizelle and I had gotten closer, and sometimes I'd hang out with Jessica and Bella.

I would soon be a senior in high school, but instead of getting a regular diploma, I'd be getting an adult education diploma. It's equivalent to the high school diploma, but with less prestige. The thought of my grade school years finally coming to an end sounded pretty darn great. I knew kids who were planning on going to a university or community college. I couldn't see myself at a university, but two years at a community college was definitely in the cards. I also had thoughts like maybe taking a break from education and just working. There were so many intriguing ideas, dreams, and possible career paths that required a college degree, though. I wavered one way and then the other, but my options were wide open. I would soon be an adult, leading a totally different kind of life. It was a lot to have to come to terms with, but at the same time, it was very exciting!

One day, while working the front counter at Jack in the Box, two decent looking guys around my age walked in. I ended up taking their order, and when one of them came to get their tray, I smiled. When they finished eating, that same boy came back up to the counter and told me that he thought I was very pretty and asked if he could take me out some time. I didn't have a boyfriend or even a guy that I was seriously talking to, so I gave him my grandma's home telephone number and they left.

Once they were gone, I couldn't help but feel really good about what just happened. I couldn't even remember the last time I went on a date. To be honest, I don't think I'd ever really had an actual date.

When I got home that night, I was anxious about this guy calling me up. My heart beat faster every time the phone rang. I was trying my hardest to stay calm so that if he did decide to call, I would sound chill and relaxed. To my pleasant surprise, he called me that same night. The conversation flowed easily and naturally from our first greetings. We talked for a good hour or so that night; I didn't want to hang up. His name was Ezekiel, and interestingly enough, he had the same last name as me: Montoya. When he told me, I couldn't help but think that if we were ever to get married, my last name would stay the same.

How boring. I had always imagined that marriage (if it ever happened for me) would mean a cool new last name.

Soon we were talking on the phone regularly, and Ezekiel invited me to his house in Azusa one night later that week. It wasn't too far from Grandma's house. He lived right across the street from the local In-N-Out Burger, where he worked.

When my grandma dropped me off at his house, we were both introduced to his mom. Later, I met his three sisters and two brothers. There was a total of six kids in his family, and no father. It must have been a lot for his mom to handle, but they were all nice—except for one. She was a little younger than me, but the eldest of the sisters. I immediately felt a cold vibe from her. It did make me feel a bit awkward about being over there, but I thought maybe she'd warm up to me if I started coming over more.

I found out that evening that Ezekiel played the guitar. He played beautifully. I told him I'd written a few songs of my own, and since I had the melody of those songs in my head, maybe he could play my melodies on his guitar and help me learn how to sing better.

When it was time for me to go, Ezekiel walked me outside. The night air was warm. He leaned in and kissed me softly and slowly; it felt amazing. I couldn't say that I knew for sure if I was going to fall for this guy—until that kiss. It was so sensual and romantic that I thought I might be falling in love then and there.

When we saw Grandma's headlights, I said goodbye to him. I felt extremely high, as if I was literally floating on a blissful cloud. Back in my bedroom, I fell asleep knowing I was headed somewhere I'd never been before, and it felt amazing.

About a week or so after our first kiss, Ezekiel asked me if I wanted to go to Disneyland with him, his best friend John, and his girlfriend. John was the other guy I met at Jack in the Box on the same day I met Ezekiel. He seemed really nice and I happily agreed. Secretly, though, I wished it was just me and Ezekiel going. Maybe he wanted his best friend's approval or something.

Whatever the reason, the outing ended up being lots of fun.

The following week, Ezekiel invited me over and we sat on the front lawn under the stars. We looked at each other for a few seconds and then he told me that he had written me a song. I couldn't believe my ears. What a fantastic surprise! As he started to play the soft, catchy melody, I felt myself embracing the moments with all my being. I had never heard him sing before, but his strong vocals began to serenade me.

> *Then a rose appeared from a garden;*
> *Mary stole my heart from me.*
> *Then a rose appeared from a garden;*
> *Mary leave your heart with me.*

I couldn't believe he was singing such a beautiful song, with lyrics meant only for me. It was by far the most romantic thing anyone had ever done for me.

From that night forward, Ezekiel was definitely my boyfriend. We became almost inseparable. When I officially introduced him to my family, everyone liked each other instantly. He always brought his guitar over to my house; he simply loved to play. That guitar was like his best friend and I imagined him becoming famous one day. I really believed in his talent. He really loved listening to Radiohead and Oasis, and he knew all their songs and played them often. One other song that he played a lot was "Where Is My Mind?" by the Pixies. I had no clue at that time who the heck they were, but I really liked that song. He also had a few of his own that he shared with me, but mostly I remember the covers.

I always kept my own personal journal of poetry and a few songs. I wrote whenever I felt inspired. I even kept a little tablet in my purse, just in case I had an idea, song or poem that I didn't want to forget. I had started this journal before I met Ezekiel, but this creative aspect was something we shared. Words, expressing emotions on paper, and the love of music helped bond us together.

As wonderful as this relationship sounds, I must admit I was still an immature, flawed teenager who didn't always treat people the way they should've been treated. I don't know why, but that's just how I was. Every time we got in an argument, I'd say, "We should break up!" I didn't know how to be a good, stable girlfriend. When we weren't arguing, I was cool, fun, chill. But I did have a bit of a temper. If anyone said or did something to me that I didn't like, they would be the first to know it.

One night, Ezekiel took me to a family friend's house, where they had six of the most adorable little black puppies ever. He told me which ones had homes waiting for them already, and which three were still up for grabs.

I never imagined that I'd be going over to someone's house to possibly adopt a puppy. I'd never had a puppy or a cat of my own before. Kitty Koo Koo was Sam and Ryan's cat, and my mom had a cat named Truffles. I wanted something that was all mine. They were mesmerizing and I had to have one. I thought about what Grandma would say, but I didn't care. I wanted my very own puppy to love and cherish.

As I was studying the pups, I noticed one curled up in a corner; he was tiny and didn't play with his brothers and sisters. They said he was a runt and would probably die without special care. My heart instantly latched on to this little guy. He needed me. He was the tiniest thing and his eyes had a bluish tint. One boy said that the tint had to do with this pup being a runt, and that he was a little sick. My new mission was to love him and make sure he didn't die. The guy told me what kind of special care the pup needed and gave me a few things that would help. He gave me a little tiny bottle and some formula, plus all the instructions I'd need. He told me that the best thing for the little guy was tender loving care. I was so ready to get him home and love the heck out of him.

While we tried to think up the perfect name, I kept calling him "little boy." I had a few suggestions, but they weren't all that good. Ezekiel told me to name him Gizmo. "He looks like Gizmo from *Gremlins*," he said.

I thought about it briefly, but wasn't totally sure that was the name I wanted to go with. But, I couldn't think of a better name, and I did like it, so Gizmo it was. Gizmo Montoya.

Ezekiel knew just as well as I did that Grandma Maria didn't know about any of this. He also knew I was afraid she'd say I couldn't keep him. I decided not to tell her. I'd sneak the pup into my bedroom and always keep my door shut. There was no lock on my door, but my grandma was cool enough to always knock before opening it. No matter what, I would never let him out of my sight. He was the size of a rat—literally. He was my little doggie rat, and I couldn't be happier.

Wrapped in a little blanket at the bottom of my purse, Gizmo stayed quiet as a mouse as I said hello to my grandma and then went straight to my room. I shut the door, leaving me and Gizmo alone for the first time—the beginning of our loving friendship. I snuck his formula into the refrigerator by wrapping it in something so my grandma wouldn't notice. I'm so lucky Grandma always knocked on my door because that little heads-up meant so much toward not getting caught. Plus, Gizmo being so small and not knowing how to bark yet made it that much easier. I knew that eventually, though, I would have to fess up.

About two weeks later, I was playing with my dog on my bedroom floor when Grandma opened my door wide. I'd been caught. Her face was priceless: pure shock. She paused for a few seconds, looking at my dog and then at me before she asked, "What's that?"

I had no choice but to tell the truth.

After explaining how, what, when, why and where I'd gotten the little guy, I had to sit there in suspense, waiting to hear what she'd say next. Before she spoke again, I told her about the love I had for Gizmo and how I'd been nursing him back to health. I should have given my grandma more credit since she's the nicest and most understanding grandmother in the world, but I couldn't help thinking she might not approve. When she said that I could keep him, I was ecstatic and relieved beyond measure. She also let me know that I would be the one to take care of him, to clean up after him, and that he would not be her responsibility. Of course, I made that promise without hesitation. That was already my intention. I had been doing fine caring for him so far. I was going to be a wonderful doggie mother.

Gizmo fit in with my family perfectly. Everyone adored him. He was the only dog in the house, so that guaranteed him lots of attention and affection. He became a little star. Everyone quickly got attached to "Gizzy." He filled a piece of my heart, spirit and soul. This animal love was much needed in my life. Having Gizmo always by my side, always knowing I would see him soon, made life so much sweeter. He even slept on my pillow every single night. We were soul mates.

When I was alone in my room, what I loved to do most was write in my poetry journal. When I wasn't doing that, I enjoyed listening to music from different genres. One song that made me feel so good and inspired me was "Breathe" by Faith Hill. When that song came out, I fell madly in love with it. I saved up to buy the CD single and then listened to it over and over again on repeat. Another slow song I loved to listen to was "Dreaming of You" by Selena. That song had been around for a while, but it never got old.

CHAPTER 17

Dangerously Reunited

Senior year at Fair Valley started off well—kind of. Something extremely unexpected happened; Dakota arrived as a new student. The idea of sharing a school with her again was a very unsettling feeling. I was still angry with her, and I knew the only reason for her transfer to Fair Valley was that her grades at Covina High must have dropped significantly since we last spoke. I'd heard that she was still partying hard, drinking, using drugs, and hanging out with Sandra and her party clan from South Hills. This was going to be totally awkward.

I avoided her as long as I could, but we ended up having a class together. I tried my best to ignore her, but it was kind of hard, and I could tell she wanted to talk to me. Then one day she just came up to me and basically told me that she wanted to be my friend again. I didn't have any close friends at Fair Valley, just a lot of acquaintances, so I couldn't help but remember the good old days. I saw in her that friend I used to like so much, and I decided to put the past behind me. I forgave her.

Meanwhile, my relationship with Ezekiel was doing okay, though not great. I suppose I was never in love with him. I loved how we were both so poetically and musically inclined. That meant a lot to me, but something else always kept me from falling completely in love with him. I had never been in love, so it's not like I knew what it felt like, but this wasn't it. What I found so exciting about our relationship was how enamored he was with me. I had never been treated so well by a guy before, and it was a beautiful thing, but back then I didn't understand just how precious it really was. I was immature, inexperienced, and if I'd known then how awful some guys could be, I would never have let him go. I should have been extremely grateful for his love, but I just didn't have the same feelings for him. Bit by bit, our relationship slipped away. Through hurtful words and actions, I subconsciously—and maybe a little consciously—pushed him further and further away.

He had a younger brother named Daniel, who was the same age as my sister Destiny. We introduced the two and they hit it off immediately. They exchanged phone numbers and began talking regularly. This new relationship between them resulted in Daniel sharing things with my sister that I would not have otherwise known about.

Destiny called me one afternoon to tell me that she'd heard Ezekiel went to Disneyland with another girl. Daniel also told her that he really liked this girl, that she had come over a couple of times and they were romantic together. I got upset when I heard this. Ezekiel was cheating on me. It turned out the girl was the drummer and the singer in his new band. I knew he was getting his first band together and he had told me that the other members were all guys, but apparently he had lied to me. Our relationship was already on the rocks, but to find out it was even worse than I thought, and in this way, still hurt.

When I confronted him, he told me that he didn't feel we were "working out" anymore, and that he really liked this new girl. I think he was relieved to tell me this. I listened. I felt weird, jealous and hurt. I wasn't in love with him, but he was still my first real boyfriend. We broke up, and I never saw him again.

Soon after that, Dakota and I were best buddies again and practically ruled Fair Valley. The past was behind us, and I was single. She was single. We loved to party. We loved to mingle. And there we were, back in the spotlight together hitting up all the parties we could.

Since I was a bit of a follower at times, Dakota could persuade me to do something that I wasn't comfortable with, or would never have considered doing on my own, even if it could get me in trouble. We stole from stores sometimes. She was more scared than I was, though, so if she asked me to steal something for her, I usually would. I became very brave when it came to theft. I had learned how to steal from the master: Stacey. So, Dakota had me take all the risks for her.

When Dakota told me she had been invited to a big house party in Long Beach, it sounded awesome. The problem was that it was about a forty-minute drive. Neither of us had a car, or a driver's license, and nobody was offering us a ride. According to Dakota, this was going to be the most happening party ever. She kept telling me about all the cool heads that were going to be there, plus all the new beach cuties that we'd never seen before. I wanted to go so badly, but I didn't think that we were going to make it.

Dakota said, "Let's take your grandma's car."

Grandma would never let me take her car; Dakota was suggesting that I steal the keys while she was sleeping. I didn't like this idea at all. In fact, it made me feel queasy. I couldn't believe she was suggesting something so devious, but she was dead serious. But then, being the careless little bitch that teenage me was, I quickly had a change of heart and agreed to it. The plan was on!

When the night of the party arrived, Grandma's phone rang around nine o'clock. It was Dakota calling to let me know it was time to leave. Grandma sat alone watching TV on the couch. I remember wondering how I was going to drive her car out of the driveway without her realizing.

"My ride's outside," I said, hanging up the phone.

Grandma smiled at me, telling me to be careful and to have a good time. I said goodbye and walked out that front door with her car keys in my purse. Never looking back or thinking twice, I shut the door behind me, walked straight to her car, and drove away.

Dakota was waiting outside her house when I picked her up. She jumped in and said, "Hell yeah! I can't believe you did it!"

Thirty-five minutes later, give or take, and after she had encouraged me to break the speed limit, we knocked on the front door of the party house. Some guy opened the door and we were handed beers right away. I didn't see many familiar faces; this was a South Hills kick back mixed with some beach heads. Dakota went to another side of the room and I was left alone to find people to mingle with. I saw a group of guys sitting on a couch, playing PlayStation. They were all taking bong rips. They offered me a hit after I went over there and started chatting, and before I knew it, I was super high. I was enjoying myself, doing my own thing, hanging out. I only saw Dakota a few times; she was walking around with some guy from South Hills, but I didn't care what she was doing. I was having a fun night out. One guy caught my attention. His name was Skyler.

Time was flying by. The fact that I had stolen my grandma's car was tucked away in the back of my mind. Being faded sure helped, and I was having such a good time talking with Skyler. Dakota came over to me when it was time to get going. I had finished a couple of beers and smoked a lot of weed. She was seriously drunk. I was not equipped to drive. I wasn't even equipped to drive sober. And I didn't want to stop talking to this boy. I hoped that he would ask for my phone number.

Everything felt cloudy as I watched Dakota saying her goodbyes, but I didn't care about saying goodbye to anyone except Skyler. I didn't want to, but I had to. Wondering if I'd ever see him again, I hugged him goodbye and then he asked for my number. I was so happy, but I tried to play it cool. When he said maybe we could hang out sometime, I have to admit I felt like I was on cloud nine.

It was two in the morning when we left. Dakota told me to go a hundred miles per hour, and I did exactly what she said. I knew it wasn't the smartest thing to do, and yet somehow I safely dropped her off at her house. All I had to do now was get myself home and hope Grandma hadn't noticed her car's absence.

I was only a few stoplights away from home when I heard sirens and saw bright lights flashing behind me.

I pulled over to the side of the road. The officer who asked for my license and registration looked like a nice man. When I said I only had my permit and didn't know where the registration was, he looked dismayed. "Is this really all you have?"

I said yes and then told him it was my grandma's car and that I took it to go to a party because my friend wanted me to. He asked if I'd been drinking, so I told him that I had two beers. Then he asked if I lived close by. I pointed to a nearby block and told him I lived there.

Fate was looking after me when that cop was the one to stop me that night. He said if he gave me a ticket it would ruin the rest of my life, and that he'd overlook the incident if I promised never to do anything like it again. Of course, I promised. He said he'd follow me home to make sure I got there safely.

Still feeling buzzed, I thanked him and started the car, then drove toward the street I'd pointed at. He stayed close behind me. I chose a house at random because all the lights were off and there was only one car in the driveway. I was playing with fire. With the nice cop still behind me, I pulled the car alongside the one in the driveway. The cop waited until I got out.

Without the time or the right mindset to take into account all that was happening, I shut the car door behind me and started walking toward the front door with my keys in my hand, then pretended to open it. My heart was racing, and I remember hoping that he wouldn't wait until I got inside. My instinct was to wave goodbye as I pretended to put my key in the door, hoping and praying that nobody who lived here would come outside and blow my cover. The officer apparently decided that I was safe at home and waved back at me before making a U-turn and driving away.

After the police car left, I quietly walked back to my grandma's car. I got inside and sat there without making a sound for about five minutes. I wanted to make sure that I would not run into that cop again. When I felt it was safe to drive away, I did. I'd never wanted to get home so badly in my life, trying my hardest to drive as perfectly and as carefully as I could to be sure I would make it home with no more stops. When I finally pulled into Grandma's driveway, I sat there for a few minutes, feeling like a magnificent blessing had been bestowed upon me. The whole night was insane and unbelievable, but it wasn't over yet.

My grandmother's bedroom light was still on. At three in the morning, that was not a good sign. I entered the house as quietly as I could, but when I shut the door and walked down the hallway, I saw Grandma sitting up in bed, reading a book. The look she gave me was the most disappointed expression I had ever seen on her. She didn't say a word, just reached out and handed me an envelope. I took it and went to my bedroom.

Alone in my room with Gizmo, I opened the envelope and found a long letter. I didn't want to read even one sentence, but I did read a few. It was heartbreaking. That letter made me feel like the worst granddaughter in the world; those words touched my heart in the saddest way.

> *I can't believe you stole my car tonight.*
> *You hurt me so bad.*
> *I've always trusted you; how could you do this to me?*

I couldn't believe that I hurt her like this. She wrote three pages detailing how badly I'd messed up. I was exhausted, and after reading the last sentence I felt I could handle, I threw the letter in my little trash can. Just like that. She must have spent at least twenty minutes writing down everything she was feeling, and I disregarded her pain so easily. I knew I'd done something terribly wrong, but I was running from her emotions as well as mine. I should have at least read what she had to say, but I didn't. I'm sorry, Grandma, for all the pain I caused you. I love you with all my life.

CHAPTER 18

Honda Prelude

Skyler called me soon after the party and we started hanging out regularly. He was a lot of fun to be around and I really dug his personality. He was nice to look at, too. We went to some parties together, and I met his folks. They were super nice, and his dad told me that I looked like Celine Dion. Another person had told me that before, too, but I never could make the comparison myself.

The Azusa Walmart was hiring, and I decided that I wanted to work there. As much as I enjoyed working at Jack in the Box, I was ready for a change. So, I applied and got the job. Bye-bye, Jack. I was a Walmart girl now.

My new job involved stocking shelves in the makeup and sanitary sections, and putting back items that had been left in shopping carts. Maybe it was the change of scenery and the new duties, but I didn't miss the drive-thru at all.

Spending time with Skyler and having Dakota in my life again forced me back into the party scene with a vengeance. I seemed to be going out every single weekend, but I would never have been so careless if I'd really understood what I was doing to myself, the scary risks I took: hitching rides with strangers, taking drugs when

I damn well pleased, and being a young, careless, wild and crazy girl. I had finally turned eighteen and, although I was technically an adult, I didn't feel or act like one.

Back at Fair Valley, I was getting good grades and looking forward to graduation. I decided to try homeschooling for the second semester of my senior year. It was a mistake. I'd meet with a teacher once a week, she'd give me my assignments, which I'd take home along with the corresponding textbooks, and then I'd turn in my work the following week. Not so hard—if I'd been as self-disciplined as I thought I was. I fell behind and didn't graduate with my class in 2000. I was disappointed in myself, but I was still dedicated to getting my diploma and only five credits away.

No matter which of my friends I was hanging out with, partying was always involved. Blazing it was an everyday thing, but Grandma didn't know about it. Nor did my mom and Sam. I don't think anyone ever knew how hardcore my life had become when I wasn't home.

Skyler and I slowly stopped talking so much. We were still cool, but we both did our own thing again. One night, while I was listening to the radio in my bedroom, I heard a commercial for Tele-Chat, a phone line where men and women could talk to one another. It seemed like a fun idea, and the cool thing was that it was free for women, but men had to pay. I enjoyed calling it because I didn't have to give any guys my phone number unless I really wanted to. I never gave Grandma's home number out to just anyone. If I wasn't interested in a guy, I could skip through their introductory message with the press of a button. I'd call in a few nights a week, usually after I got home late from work.

Grandma would pick me up from Walmart and we'd pick up dinner, often swinging through my old Jack in the Box drive-thru on the way home. Then she would stay up with me for a little while and watch TV before she retired to her bedroom to read until she fell asleep. Once she was in her bedroom, I would sneak out to the side of the house and smoke a couple hits of weed out of an apple. I liked using an apple because it gave it a little flavor. Plus, I didn't own my own pipe. Then, I'd go to my room and call Tele-chat. I talked quietly, and it never seemed to disturb my grandma. I wasn't calling the line because I really wanted to meet someone. If that happened, it would be cool, but I simply enjoyed passing the time, talking away for fun.

Most nights, though, I'd come home from work, do the same thing with the apple and weed, then watch *The Tonight Show with Jay Leno* and then *Late Night with Conan O'Brian*. I'd watch these shows from my grandma's couch, stoned and laughing away. I absolutely loved those shows: pure jokes and laughter, though being high as a kite probably made it even funnier.

Things changed a little when Uncle Gary needed a place to stay for a couple of months. There were three bedrooms in her house, one of which would now be occupied by him. I was still going out with my friends, smoking, drinking, and had even added something new to my regimen: cigarettes. Not smart, I know, but I didn't always do the smartest of things. For so long, I'd say, "Why would I smoke cigarettes when they could kill me, but don't even do anything fun to your mind? Smoking weed doesn't kill you, and it *does* do something fun to your mind."

Basically, getting high without causing harm to my health was way better than not getting high and harming my health. I never understood why people chose to smoke those tobacco sticks, and now I was one of them. All the popular people smoked at parties, so it seemed like something I should incorporate into my lifestyle.

Now that my uncle was staying with us, I wasn't calling Tele-Chat as much. I became more self-conscious about using the home phone because he also had an extension in his room. How weird and embarrassing it would be if he were to pick up the phone and listen in or something! I'm sure I was being paranoid, but nevertheless, I wasn't going to take that chance. If I'd owned a cell phone back then, it would have been a different story. I'm not saying I never called. Uncle Gary would often leave the house at night to go chill up in the mountains or whatever else he did with his time, so I did have a safe window to safely be on the phone.

One night while I was on the line, I ended up talking with this guy that I got really interested in. It was the first time this ever happened on Tele-Chat. His name was Keith.

I never gave out my real name on the chat line. I always used aliases like Haley, Brianna or Skylene. I'm positive the name I gave Keith was Haley. We talked for a few hours and exchanged phone numbers at the end of the night.

Keith started calling me a few times a week. He was twenty-eight—ten years older than me—and lived by Magic Mountain in the Santa Clarita Valley—an hour away from me. After a few weeks of talking regularly, he suggested getting together. Despite the risks involved in a blind date, I was totally down for it. I didn't have a car, so he was going to drive down and pick me up.

I told Grandma about it, though I left out the part about meeting this guy on a telephone chat line. Instead, I made up a story, and I might have lied about how old he was. She was fine with it.

When the day of our date arrived, I was nervous of course, but I was also really excited. Keith arrived in the middle of the afternoon. After hearing the long-awaited knock, I anxiously opened the door. I was relieved to find that I felt attracted to him, and his expression said he felt the same way. I invited him in to meet my grandma, and after a few minutes we left for what would end up being a fun time.

He took me to a restaurant, and we were really hitting it off. Afterward, we went to an old town shopping area to walk, talk and laugh. It was nice. He was a gentleman. Once we got back to my grandma's house, we sat outside in his parked car and talked for about twenty minutes. Finally, he went in for a kiss, and I gladly kissed him back. We made out for a couple of minutes, then said our goodbyes.

After that, we both wanted to hang out together as much as we could. It sucked that he lived so far away. We did see each other again, but it always entailed him driving an hour or more, depending on traffic, to pick me up. During this time period, I had moved back home with my family. We would always hang out in my neighborhood, until one day he picked me up and asked if I wanted to go to his house. When I agreed, he asked if I'd be able to stay the night and I told him yes. Keith assumed I would tell my mom what I was doing, but I didn't.

Keith's house was small, but had a front and a backyard. It was definitely the right size for a bachelor. He showed me around, then we chilled and went out to get some dinner. I ended up spending the night there, and my family had no idea where I was. I was being very immature and feeling goofy, inconsiderate and mean, so the next day, when I finally decided to call mom's house, my sister Destiny answered and I did something I still can't believe or explain. Making my voice sound fearful and shaky, I said, "Help me. Help me."

"Rosemary, where are you?"

"I'm at someone's house and I don't know where."

Destiny sounded scared to death. "Rose, are you okay?"

"I don't know. Help me."

"Rose, what should I do?"

"Help me," I said one last time before hanging up the phone. Thinking what I had just done was funny, I went back to my day with Keith as if nothing had happened.

That night, I thought about what I'd told my sister on the phone earlier, and figured I should call her again and check in. This time I would let her know everything was alright and I was only joking with her.

When I called the house, my sister Alyssa answered the phone. "Rosemary, you're ok? Everyone's been worried sick about you! We thought you were kidnapped."

"Oh no!" I said, as if I didn't know that what I had done earlier would drive everybody into a frenzy. Alyssa told me that Mom, Destiny and Ryan had gone to the Tele-Chat office in Los Angeles to try and find me, and all they had was an address. She told me to have Keith drive me over there to meet them.

I immediately told Keith about the prank call I'd made, and, using his internet connection, we were able to find the Tele-Chat address. I called Mom's cell phone right away.

She answered in the saddest voice I ever heard. "Hello?"

"Mommy, I'm okay," I said.

"Rosemary, is that you?"

"Yes."

"Thank God you're alright!" Gently sobbing with relief, she asked, "Where are you?"

I let her know that I was in my friend's car and that we were driving to meet her. She pulled over and gave me an address with cross streets. Keith knew exactly where to go.

Once we saw her car, Keith and I hurried up and said our goodbyes. He parked behind Mom; she looked like a nervous wreck. I saw my brother crying in the back seat, and my sister Destiny sat there with a face swollen from tears. I felt awful for the prank. Mom was just so happy I was alive. She told me how all she could imagine was that I'd been raped and left for dead in a ditch or an alley somewhere. As inconsiderate as I was back then, I still felt her pain. Sam had assured Mom that I was going to turn up fine. Mom hoped he was right and told him that if I did, he could ground me for as long as he wanted. Once we got home, Sam expressed how angry he was with me and grounded me hardcore. I accepted my punishment wholeheartedly. I knew I deserved it, and that I couldn't hurt my family like this ever again.

I continued to see Keith. He'd still drive down to meet me when he was available. He worked full-time and I still did my homeschooling and kept up my part-time job at Walmart. Our relationship became kind of serious.

He drove a bright blue truck, but there was a dark blue Honda Prelude parked in his driveway that he said he was planning to fix up and get back on the road.

I had recently gotten my driver's license. No more permit. It felt good. I didn't have a car yet, but I knew how to drive an automatic pretty well. I'd already had lots of practice in Grandma's car, and I'd driven my mom's car a decent amount, too.

Then Keith gave me his Honda Prelude. He wanted me to drive to his house sometimes, which made sense. The only problem was that the Honda was a stick shift. Not only had I never driven a stick shift before, but I had a feeling that I didn't think I could ever learn to drive that kind of car—nor did I want to. I only felt comfortable with automatics.

Mom told me that her first car was a stick and how she actually preferred it. It gave her something to do while driving, she said. I think Keith knew that this gift was not that desirable to me, and the more I thought about taking it, the less I wanted it. But I didn't want to seem ungrateful. Keith wanted to split the driving with me. It would have been rude not to take the car.

He gave me a few lessons before I officially took it, but no matter how hard I tried, I never really got the hang of it. I bought an "it's all about me" bumper sticker and slapped it right on the bumper. Later, I got another bumper sticker that read, "Got beer?" I wasn't even 21 yet. Even if I was, that's not the type of attention someone wants drawn to themselves. It screams, "Pull me over! See if I'm drunk, and maybe I can get a DUI!"

February 17, 2001, was just another ordinary day. I'd been driving the Honda for almost two weeks and I'd already driven my sisters, brother, and a few friends around town. Everyone thought it was so dope. My sister Destiny and I decided to take a ride down to Mom's See's Candies store at the Brea Mall and have lunch with her. It would be the first time we'd ever done this. Mom was still a manager and had recently started running the Brea Mall shop. She gave us directions that were easy to follow.

We got there fine, and the three of us had a bite to eat at an Auntie Anne's located right next to See's. We sat and visited until her lunch break was over. When Mom had to go back to work, we hugged her goodbye, did a little window-shopping, got into the Honda, and drove away.

CHAPTER 19

Boom

Everything seemed cool as we got onto the freeway to head home. Des and I sang along to "Ain't No Fun" by Snoop Doggy Dog. Mom told us that as soon as we got onto the freeway, we would need to transfer over to the 57. I don't know why, but I got confused when the moment arrived and got onto the 71 Corona Freeway instead. I don't remember ever being on that road before. Things suddenly started to feel strange. The song blasting next through the car stereo was "Add It Up" by the Violent Femmes. We loved that song and were feeling its vibes, but something just didn't feel right. Somehow, we ended up in the fast lane.

The sun was setting. We knew we needed to get off at the next exit because we had no idea where the heck we were going. But before we could do that, the Prelude stalled right there in the fast lane. I kept trying to start the car up again and again, but nothing. We sat there in that dead car with traffic flying past us. I opened the driver's side door, got out, and started waving, directing cars to go around us. An oncoming car in the distance was hurtling toward us at full speed, as if the driver couldn't see me standing there. Destiny shouted at me to get back inside the car. I slowly started to sit down in my seat. That's the last thing I remember.

Destiny had to tell me the next part of the story. She was coherent after the crash and said that I froze when she screamed at me to get in the car and put on my seatbelt. We were hit hard from behind, and the car surged forward. Destiny frantically looked over at the driver's side, but didn't see me. In fact, the empty seat was bent up against the steering wheel.

Looking all around and then ahead at the freeway, she saw me lying in the carpool lane, my body mangled. One of my legs was positioned up over my head. Terrified, Destiny couldn't believe what she was seeing; her sister was all twisted up and bleeding out onto the asphalt. She thought I was dead.

Passing cars slowed down to look at the wreck, before the police and paramedics arrived. Most people stayed in their vehicles, but there were a few who got out and were attentive to my sister. A lady tried to comfort her. Everyone in sight felt horrible because my condition didn't look hopeful. Destiny, completely shaken, was able to use that lady's cell phone to call Mom at work.

Mom picked up. "Thanks for calling See's Candies. How may I help you?"

Destiny held the cell phone, barely able to speak as police officers and paramedics began to arrive on the scene.

"Destiny, is everything alright?"

Crying and fighting hard to catch her breath, Destiny told Mom that we were in a bad car accident.

"Are you okay?"

"Yes."

"Is Rosemary okay?"

Sobbing, Destiny looked over at me sprawled out in the carpool lane. "Well... She moved."

I guess even in my unconscious state, my body was able to move, to twitch. Destiny handed the phone back to the lady, who gave Mom our exact location. Mom dropped everything and rushed to our rescue.

Once she was on the freeway, Mom drove along the shoulder lane all the way to the accident. Traffic was at a standstill, with police officers controlling the flow. When Mom finally arrived at the scene, there were only two officers left. I was in such critical condition that a helicopter had been ordered to airlift me to the Loma Linda trauma unit. An ambulance took Destiny to a nearby hospital on a stretcher.

The officers told Mom to take pictures of both vehicles. The Prelude was destroyed; it had been pushed forward twenty-five feet and shattered glass was scattered all around. I had been ejected through the open door and thrown thirty feet into the carpool lane. There was a certain angelic twist to the wreckage; the back seats were smashed up against the front seats. If anyone had been sitting back there, they would surely have been crushed. Then there was my seat, which had ended up practically on top of the steering wheel. If I had been safely buckled in, I would have been crushed, too. The most amazing part of it all was that my sister's seat was untouched. It was still in the same position and condition that it had been in before the accident. Destiny did have her seatbelt on, and was not badly injured apart from some severe whiplash. Considering everything that could've happened, she walked away with minor physical injuries.

As horrible as my situation was, at least I wasn't crushed in that front seat. I honestly don't think I'd be alive today if my seatbelt had been secured like it should have been. I know I can't prove anything, but I feel that some unseen powerful force had to be with us that day.

CHAPTER 20

Coma

Phone calls, hospital, frantic worry, troubled hearts, tears, horror, disbelief. Everyone in my family tried to make sense of what happened and why. No one could understand. My life and all it entailed was in the universe's hands.

When Mom arrived at the trauma unit, I was already undergoing an emergency surgery on my right knee. Two ligaments were torn: the PCL and the ACL. They were only able to reconstruct one of them at the time. I was in a medically induced coma, with no updates on my condition. It would be a waiting game for anyone who loved me.

Sam, Grandma Maria, and other members of my family joined Mom at the hospital, waiting for news. No one was able to see me yet. They all knew about my knee surgery, the coma, and that I had a head injury, but no more than that. No one knew whether or not I'd survive.

At some point, a doctor explained to my mother that I had suffered a severe traumatic brain injury. No one could tell its full extent at that point. He told Mom I might be mentally challenged for the rest of my life, that I might be a vegetable, never again able to speak or be fully aware. He said I might have amnesia, or mental and physical disabilities, that the problems could last a short time, or they could be permanent. Until I woke up, no one could say for sure. And, of course, there was a final possibility—I might never wake up.

The waiting game continued. After a while, the doctor allowed a few people in to see me. Mom and Sam were first. Mom cried and held my hand while she prayed for me.

After I'd been in a coma for two days, Mom and Sam came again. Right away, Mom noticed I didn't have the breathing machine tubes hooked up anymore. I was still in a coma, but I was able to breathe on my own. Then, something magical happened.

Sam was crying, telling me, "I love you, Rose-mo." That was a nickname he had for me.

Mom, sobbing with grief, told me, "I love you, Rosemary."

In a clear voice, I replied, "I love you, too."

I stayed in that coma for one more day without saying another word, but Mom knew then that I wouldn't be a vegetable or mentally challenged. She felt it was a sign telling her that everything would be ok. That connection I made with her gave her the comfort she so desperately needed. After that, she was a believer in something greater beyond the human realm. She was so thankful.

A day later, I started showing signs of responsive activity. I began mumbling words. They made no sense, but at least I was talking. Mom was called in and she rushed to my bedside.

This is when my conscious memory started to come back. I remember most of what happened from that moment on, even though I was very much out of it and barely coherent.

A man's voice said, "Can you feel me touching your fingers?"

Unable to open my eyes, I dazedly mumbled, "Yes."

"How many fingers am I squeezing?"

I don't remember if I answered all his questions correctly, but I do remember him saying that I'd done a good job when he was finished.

Everything felt surreal and strange. I had no clue what was going on. When I couldn't do what was being asked of me anymore, the doctor would finish up and tell me to get some rest. It took a lot of strength and energy to do what he asked of me, but I know that I had never tried harder at anything.

A few days later, my eyes opened more and more. The doctor administered more tests. I could only handle so many questions before I had nothing left to say and my eyes would droop.

He'd tell me, "It's okay; you've done enough for today. Go ahead and rest. I'll see you tomorrow."

The doctor made me feel comfortable, and there was a woman with him during every session. He would tell her to talk sometimes. She sounded lovely and very familiar. Later, I'd find out it was my mom. She told me that my first words when I was finally fully awake were, "Can I have a cigarette?"

I guess I was addicted. Wow. That still astonishes me today. Cigarettes are some deeply rooted scary-ass mind control sticks.

A week or so later, it seemed I was doing well, all things considering. Another patient and I even saw a teacher for twenty minutes a day. They wanted me to be involved in some study they were doing over a long period of time. The doctor finally felt that I didn't need to be at the trauma unit anymore, and soon I was transferred to San Dimas Hospital. Destiny rode in the ambulance with me. Mentally, I was in another world, but I recall telling a paramedic he was cute and then talking a bunch of gibberish. The guy kept smiling, along with my sister. My barely coherent crazy talk went on; every day I seemed to be a little more aware of my surroundings, but understanding what was actually happening was a totally different story.

After the first week, I sort of knew who my mom and sisters were, but one day, when my brother and my cousin Michael visited, I thought my cousin was my brother and my brother was my cousin. You could've told me that my name was Marilyn Monroe, that I was a famous actress, and that the year was 1952, and I would have believed you. Fortunately, no one lied to me. They all kept telling me my name, my age, and whatever else they could to help me remember a little bit more of who I was. I believed whatever I was told, but really, I was just listening, and trying to comprehend anything was extremely difficult. I pretty much let everything go in one ear and out the other without even meaning to.

It felt like I had absolutely zero attention span. I kept talking and talking, never knowing when to shut up, and I laughed all the time. Most of the time nothing was actually funny, but for some reason, to me, so many things were just hilarious. People would smile at me while I had a blast with myself in my incoherent mind. I was like a five-year-old; I knew how to speak clearly, but that's all. I didn't understand reality for what it was. I was in my own fun house, in my own fun land.

Mom was my guide. She had to tell me to quiet down if I was getting too carried away. For the most part, she let me be the crazy accident Rosemary I was, but when enough was enough Mom would gently steer me in a different direction. I could talk to visitors for days, carrying on with my nonsense for far too long while Mom gestured in the background for me to stop talking. There were a bunch of different stages I had to go through during the mental healing process, and if I had to estimate how many my brain endured, I'd guess thirty. The mind is the most insanely complex and powerful thing imaginable—and it can certainly be very scary.

After a week at Loma Linda, and a couple of weeks at San Dimas Hospital, I was transferred to my third and final facility: Queen of the Valley in West Covina. Coincidentally, it was the same hospital I was born in.

I had many visitors. Pastor Bernald and his wife, friends of my grandma, came, and so did other members of Calvary Lutheran church, where Grandma had been president for more than twenty years. Many of those people had known me since my childhood, and were present when my sister Alyssa and I were baptized together. A few of my mother's friends visited, and a few of mine did, too. They would all tell me how sorry they were for the accident I was in, but I didn't understand what they were talking about because I was still confused about what was going on and who I was.

The doctor at Queen of the Valley told Mom to bring me any old papers, journals, music, pictures and memorabilia of any kind in the hopes that it might spark some memories. She did bring pictures, but the most precious thing she brought was my poetry journal. I longed to see my dog Gizmo. When I remembered him, I begged Mom to bring him to me. The doctor said it would be okay and I'll never forget the day Mom brought Gizmo into my room. I was so happy and overjoyed to see him, and you could tell he felt the same way. I hugged him tightly. He lay beside me for a while. We cuddled and loved.

When Gizzy needed to go home, I couldn't wait to be with him every day again. I was left alone to look over my journal. At the time, I didn't have the brain capacity to read and comprehend any of it. Later that night, Mom read me some of it, but it didn't sound familiar.

It was hard to remember who I was, and it was going to take some time to recover. I was lucky to have my mom and such loving people around to help me. The funny thing is, I kept asking for a cigarette. Finally, the doctor gave in and let me have one. Mom wheeled me outside to smoke it. I could only take a few hits because it made me feel lightheaded beyond belief. There were so many things that I couldn't remember—too bad I had to remember I smoked cigarettes.

CHAPTER 21

Going Home

The day finally came for me to go home. I still wasn't exactly sure where that was, only that it sounded wonderful. Good old Shadydale Avenue. I felt safe and sound at home in Covina. Mom had a lot on her plate to deal with—as if she hadn't before. To think that her oldest daughter should have been almost ready to start a new life fresh out of high school, that those rough parenting years would soon be behind her, only to find that instead, she had to take care of me again.

"Mommy!" I yelled. "Where's my journal?"

After a few days of being settled in at home in my old room, I felt like skimming through the pages. Mom looked around the house briefly and realized that it wasn't there. She called the hospital right away to ask if we'd left it behind and was told that my room had been cleaned out for a new occupant and they didn't know where it could be. I didn't know that losing that journal would leave such a hole in my heart one day.

I lived every day from then on going through bizarre mental stages. The first stage was extremely confusing. I had zero attention span and I never knew when to shut up, relax, eat, or think for myself on any sane level. I was incoherent, a mental mess. My temperament and way of processing things was all haywire. There was one awful, disturbing feeling that I was forced to deal with 24/7. It was a big cloud that covered my whole brain, and every morning, I'd wake up feeling smothered by this cloud. It was so bothersome that Mom made an appointment with the neurologist.

My neurologist told me things about my brain injury that I had never known. He began by telling me how lucky I was to have this type of injury, and at the same time how unlucky I was. My brain wasn't fractured, which was good for my recovery process, but it was so badly bruised that he compared it to a bad earthquake. The cells had been knocked all over the place. Everything in there had been misplaced. Every second, every minute, every hour of every day, my brain would be healing. I would notice little changes each month, but more significant changes would be measured yearly. It would take a long time, but everything that had been knocked around would eventually start to correct itself—like connecting the dots. In time, the cells would find their way back home.

He went on to tell me that this kind of brain injury would make me feel worse for many years before I started feeling better, and that someone who had suffered a more devastating brain injury with no chance of recovering would never know the difference, and therefore would find it easier to accept. As for me, I would be conscious of my injury, but have no control over it. It would feel like I was trapped in another person's mind. A horrifying reality to live through: little did I know that this annoying cloud was my only protection from that reality.

But the cloud would one day dissipate and leave. I was told that, in a year or two, I would literally wake up one morning and it would be gone. That is when the new "reality" would take place: Stage 2 of the recovery process. Time was all that could heal my bruised brain. It would be a long waiting game of ten to twelve years for my brain to fully heal itself. Even then, my brain would continue to restore itself for the rest of my life.

It sounded like a long time, but given the fact that my sense of time and space was all off anyway, it didn't bother me that much. All I knew was what my doctor told me, and it stuck to the core of my brain like superglue. Hearing about the chance of being normal again one day gave me great hope and determination. That doctor had no idea what a positive impact he had on me. I'm sure my mom didn't, either. I'd hold that news close to my heart and lean on it whenever times got tough. That news was my fighting power. Every day, I dreamed of a healed version of myself.

In the meantime, I had to rehabilitate my right knee, which wouldn't bend at all at first. Mom took me to physical therapy three or four days a week. It was painful and took a lot of work. I'd push my hardest, but when the pain got too severe, I had to stop. Without my Vicodin, I don't think I could have done it.

Every night, Mom had to help bathe me. I could wash most of my body, but she would have to wash my legs and feet. Dr. Baldwin ordered a special shower bench for me. Mom and Sam also had to install a showerhead with a moveable hose.

Mealtimes were always hard for me; I would mostly talk, not eat. That attention span and the overtalking thing were really big issues for me. As most people are aware, the slower you eat, the fuller you feel and the less you actually eat. It's an ideal way to lose weight, but I only weighed eighty pounds and needed to gain weight. The problem was that I loved to talk, and quite simply didn't know when to shut up. Most of the time I would end up eating only a quarter of my meal. Mom would watch me as I ate and use hand gestures and verbal instructions to get me to stop talking and eat. Sadly, her advice rarely registered.

I can only imagine now how hard this must have been for my family, to see their sister and daughter acting and looking so differently than the girl they grew up with.

During a physical therapy session later that year, the most amazing thing happened. I was on the exercise bike, and before I knew it, I was pedaling full revolutions with my right leg. This was the day I'd been waiting for. I called joyfully for my mom to come see. I felt like the happiest, proudest girl ever, like I had reached this big milestone. Mom was just as happy as me and as I kept riding, we started crying. We had done this together. It was a beautiful moment.

I got a big treat that night thanks to my sister Destiny. Once a week, or once every other week, we'd go to a Barnes & Noble bookstore in West Covina. These were the most fun outings we shared, and to this day I don't think I've ever laughed so hard as I did during those trips. Mom would drop us off there in the early evening and come back two hours later to pick us up. Once we got inside, we'd get coffee or a smoothie from the Starbucks kiosk, then head straight for the animal books section. We'd laugh just looking at all the book covers, then grab a few and find a space on the floor to flop down, chill, and look through them. I suppose in my injured, immature mind, and with my sister being young herself, it made sense we'd find those pictures of animals so damn amusing. Not just kind of funny, but madly hilarious.

Every page we looked at made me point and burst out laughing. Whatever animal it was, and whatever pose it was in just made us laugh uncontrollably. The animals' faces did it for me, to the point where I would be laid out on the floor cracking up so hard that my stomach would start hurting. I don't know why I found it all so amusing, except my injured brain absolutely did. Laughter surely is the best medicine.

I was still in my brace, and a guy I had met on the chat line wanted to meet me in person. So, I told him how my sister and I would be at Barnes & Noble one night. We were there, drinking coffee, laughing, and doing the usual for about half an hour before the guy showed up. I looked up and saw a guy holding a Starbucks cup, and he appeared to be looking for someone. He didn't look much like how I'd imagined he would, but I couldn't help but think that this might be him. When we made eye contact, he walked over and asked if I was Rosemary. When I said yes, he bent down to our level to ask what we were doing.

I didn't even care that he was there trying to meet and talk to me; I continued laughing and turning the pages of whatever book I was looking at. He found it odd that I was laughing so hysterically at pictures of animals, but I just didn't care. Then again, I didn't care what anyone thought. I was just happy and content in my own little world. As he kept trying to talk to me, I continued looking at the fun animal books. Eventually I realized I should talk to him a bit, even though I wasn't at all interested. I couldn't ignore him completely, so after five minutes or so I asked what kind of coffee he was drinking. When he answered that it was black, I lost it. Somehow, I thought this was the most hilarious thing in the world, and spit the coffee in my mouth all over this guy's white shirt.

When I finally caught my breath, I apologized profusely. My sister couldn't help but giggle. I could tell he was upset, and I kept apologizing as he tried to hide his anger. He asked why I did that and what was so funny. I told him I'd never heard of anyone that drank their coffee pure black and it was funny to me. Then I told him how me, my family, and friends all drink it with at least cream or sugar, if not both, and when he said his coffee was just black, I lost all control. He still didn't get it, but he chatted with us for another fifteen minutes or so before I guess he felt it wasn't working out and decided to leave. Destiny and I laughed so hard after he left and continued with our night of fun, jokes, and pure laughter.

CHAPTER 22

Meeting the Accident Rosemary

About a year and a half later, I woke up one morning as I always did: with my little black terrier poodle by my pillow. It should have been an average day in my world, except it wasn't. The cloud was gone!

I couldn't believe it. I felt so different, and a lot clearer. I yelled to my mom, and she came running. I told her over and over how my cloud had lifted. "It's gone, it's gone!" I sang. She was happy because I was so happy. It felt really good, yet really strange. And it happened precisely the way the doctor said it would. It's amazing how right on he was.

I felt a lot clearer, and not having a cloudy substance covering my brain was a good thing. At the same time, things were starting to make more sense to me. I was more aware of what was happening around me, and inside my mind. It was disturbing, and soon I didn't like the uneasy feelings I was having. Everything around me looked and felt more real. Fear, worry and reality automatically set in. I suddenly realized just how abnormal I was. I knew I was messed up before, but it was sort of okay. It was just the way of life. My problems hadn't felt like problems. Now they did. And I felt further away from myself than I ever had before.

The new me sucked. It was such a creepy disgusting feeling. I remembered the sane Rosemary before the accident and began calling her "the old Rosemary." I came to call this new, brain-injured Rosemary, "the accident Rosemary." I knew and felt with all my soul that the two were completely different. The old Rosemary had abandoned me and replaced herself with some crazy, stupid, mildly coherent, weird, mentally unbalanced Rosemary.

I was still wild, but I'd calmed down a lot since I was now more aware. But it wasn't a good reality. Who was this new girl? Why did this happen to her? It was hell. I felt trapped in a really ugly part of the old Rosemary's mind. At the same time, I remembered all the wonderful things about the old Rosemary, but I couldn't touch her. She was only a memory of a great girl I once knew.

The accident Rosemary was not wonderful, or even the least bit good. She was everything the old Rosemary wasn't. As much as I disliked this Rosemary, as much as I didn't understand her, and as much as I wanted her and all her craziness to go away and never come back, I was stuck with her. Ten years, the doctor had said it might take for her to come back to me. That felt like forever. I started to live for the day, and often daydreamed about the day she'd return.

Waking up each morning and falling asleep each night was a blessing in disguise. I lived on an up and down roller coaster through a maze of strange thoughts and emotions I could never control. I was hostage to the games my mind played on me. I felt like a prisoner trapped in my own mind, trying to find my way out. My family was still there like always, but my long lost best friend, the old Rosemary, was not. I knew one sweet day she'd find me and I would be waiting with open arms. Every single day I imagined that glorious reunion.

But that reunion wouldn't take place for a very long time. So, I was angry. The pain and anguish I felt was often too much to bear.

No one could help me through this. The only thing that could possibly help was time: lots and lots of time. I never really lived for the day or embraced it for its true worth. I only looked forward to the future, and lived through the present.

During all this craziness, I also underwent a series of surgeries for a new front tooth. The first, a bone graft surgery, was the worst. I'd lost too much bone in the accident, so the oral surgeon had to take bone from my chin and implant it above where my new tooth was going. After that surgery, my whole face was black and blue, and puffed out like a chipmunk. It hurt, and I looked so injured for about two months before most of the bruising healed.

The second surgery was six months later and easier than the first, but still painful. After another six months, I had my final surgery. I was told this one would be the easiest and least painful of all. I was still put under anesthesia and given pain pills afterward, but there was no bruising and at the end of it I had a beautiful new front tooth. My oral surgeon did an excellent job; they called him the Picasso of teeth because he was so artistic. It sure beat having to wear a fake flipper tooth with Polident to hold it up, and having to take it out every night. It was all worth it.

I still didn't know what to do with all the anger running through my veins, so I decided to buy a journal to write all my feelings in. I needed an outlet, an escape, something to pour all my anger out into. This journal would be the complete opposite of the one I left at the hospital, because this would be about death, hatred, anger, and yelling at God.

> *God, you're so evil and mean!*
> *There is no God, or God is the devil.*
> *How could you do this to me?*
> *How horrible are you to make me feel this way?*

I would write down exactly how I felt, and what I wanted to do to myself. It was all so horrible and awful; nothing made any sense and I wanted out of my crazy mind. I hated myself and I wanted to die. They were pages full of horror—all deathly, dark poems. It was my journal of pain. I wrote down my hatred for God and for myself, how stupid I was, and I asked why I was even living. I hated God for making me this way. I hated every part of the way I felt, thought and looked.

I was also way too skinny, but I couldn't gain any weight. I went up to ninety pounds at most. But nothing surpassed the mental horror I was in. No matter how many surgeries I would have to undergo, or how much physical pain I was in, my mental state was by far the worst of all.

And I was pretty much done with the surgeries, too. It would be up to me if I wanted the last ligament in my knee reconstructed. At the time, I didn't think I wanted another knee surgery. I had a pronounced limp when I walked, but I knew I didn't want to have to learn to walk all over again after having another surgery. Dr. Baldwin told me I could have my other ligament reconstructed at any time, but if I chose to go through with it there was still a chance my limp wouldn't go away. This surgery would be cosmetic. The scariest part was that Dr. Baldwin only gave me an eighty percent chance that my profound limp would go away. It was a gamble. Sure, the odds were in my favor, but I couldn't help but think the worst.

Dealing with my mind was hell enough. Did I really want to add to the struggle? I chose to not go through with it. The door was always open if I ever changed my mind.

When I think about all the surgeries I'd had, all the pain, the weight loss, the scars on my face, the mental torment was the worst part. I would suffer through twenty more surgeries if I could have my mind back. My mind was connected to my well-being as a whole, and I didn't have that to back up all the other efforts I was making to recover.

And there's something else I have to confess to. Trying to release some of my extreme anger, hatred and depression, I started cutting myself. I liked cutting my arms and sometimes my legs because I really felt that pain. I liked hurting myself. I hated myself so much and felt so much mental turmoil that I tried my hardest to make instant physical pain match my mental pain. It might not have worked out quite the way I'd intended, but it did help a little with the frustration and released some suppressed anger. I knew not to cut any crucial veins; as much as I felt like dying at times, I was scared to actually die. But I would cut away at myself until I felt satisfied with the amount of pain I caused.

I didn't know about meditation or other calming techniques. Even if I had, I didn't have the attention span and patience to be still long enough. I did have a dog, though. He kept me on my feet, walking, which was a great help. Walking is also a form of meditation, and a great form of exercise that is great for the mind. Never underestimate the wonderful power of walking. The benefit of body movement through light exercise is fantastic: great for the mind, body, spirit and soul. Having an animal in your life is another form of therapy all in itself. So, I did have some help, but nothing exactly worked wonders for me back then.

I felt like I'd entered a third stage of recovery about six months after the cloud lifted. There had been just enough time for me to become accustomed to my new state of mind and its neurotic, insane way of processing things. Everything around me was strange and different, and I felt odd around family and friends. I never talked about it; I wouldn't have known how. People could see some abnormalities for themselves.

But I wasn't always in the pit of despair. Thinking was still a challenge for me, but I tried to have fun the best way I knew how. As long as I was entertained, I'd get lost in my mind. Trips to Barnes & Noble with my sister Destiny were still a form of therapy for me. I was still able to keep that crazy, laughing part of myself going at times.

This new recovery stage gave way to many more strange thoughts, which I had yet to experience. One day will always stand out for me as an example of how weak and absurd my mind was. I'd spent the day with Grandma Maria and my dog Gizmo. Gizmo often tagged along wherever I'd go. We were all driving back from somewhere, and Grandma needed to stop by her house. She had me and Gizzy wait in the car. Five minutes passed, then fifteen, then almost thirty minutes. We were waiting in that car for such a long time, and besides Gizmo, I had nothing but my thoughts to distract me. That was not a good thing.

While we waited, I could hear Grandma and Uncle Gary, who still lived there, talking. Sitting restlessly in that car led my mind to some horribly disturbed musings. A thought came to me—just one single thought. That's all it was. But I had to go along with it, even though it was so ridiculous. I could try my hardest to overcome what was terrorizing me, but it didn't matter because I wasn't in control. If my mind wanted to grab onto a thought, then it would always be a lost battle for me. On this particular day, the thought my mind wanted to torment me with was, *What if someone put a spell or curse on me so that I'd never be able to talk again?*

It sounds ridiculous, absurd. Why would anyone entertain such a stupid thought? This brain-injured girl would. I mean, this thought really screwed with my head, and it affected my whole being in no time.

I knew from the moment that the thought entered my mind that I was going to be held captive by it for a long time. A large part of my mind took it seriously, and then it started to take over the rest like a successful bank robber takes over a bank's entire cash flow. But, I still had this small, logical voice in some lost cell in my brain and in my heart asking how this could be. My mind was so disorganized, so disrupted, and so out of touch with reality that this thought was pure destruction for poor, incapable accident Rosemary.

I felt so sorry for her. I was living as that Rosemary, but I still remembered the old Rosemary. I was unable to connect the logical dots even though somewhere deep down I knew this shouldn't be bothering me the way it was. I was stuck. I was lost. I was prey to my injured brain.

So, being in that car for half an hour with Gizmo was going to change my life—again. When Grandma finally came back, it felt like it had been hours. It hadn't, but it was too long to have been left alone with my untamed mind. Sometimes I wonder whether that obsessive thought would have ever come to my mind if I hadn't been left in that car all that time. I guess I'll never know. Subconsciously, that thought was a sensitive issue for me, and now I would be dealing with it indefinitely. If not that thought, then some other one would've eventually grabbed me. The extreme weakness of my mind was bound to be let loose sooner or later.

When we drove away, I was a nervous wreck. I felt unstable, misaligned, and more unwell then before. I never told her, but if she only knew what had gone down while she was away. Then again, even if she did know, it wouldn't have mattered. The only way I could escape my mental prison was by the passing of time—lots of time—or death.

CHAPTER 23

Medication

Things had been bad enough before, but now I was terrorized by this obsessive thought. It got so bad that I ended up telling Mom, even though in some deep down, lost brain cell I knew the idea was ludicrous. Telling her was probably a cry for help, and it certainly worked because she called my neurologist, who told her that I should see a psychiatrist, and she made an appointment right away.

The psychiatrist asked whether I'd ever experienced obsessive thoughts before my accident. I told him how there were a few times, but they'd been so mild that they didn't affect my life or my well-being. He said that any little problems I might have had before my accident would now be greatly intensified. Little things that would not have bothered me before would likely become too much to bear. There would be changes in the way I processed things while my brain was healing, he said. Having a doctor who understood what I was experiencing made seeing a psychiatrist very helpful.

The office was only about two miles away from our house. He listened to my story and prescribed an anti-depressant called Prozac and an anti-anxiety pill called Ativan. Prozac was the best pill for OCD, and helped control my anxiety levels as well as the depression. The Ativan should help when experiencing extreme anxiety, he'd said.

I was lucky in that neither of the prescribed drugs had any negative side effects on me, but the Ativan had no effect at all. He then switched me to Xanax, which did the trick. After about two weeks, I felt a little better, and after a month, I was coping much better with my problems. I was still far from being well, but the intensity and frequency of depression, anger and anxiety had been reduced.

I still had gross, ugly feelings at times, because there was no pill that could take away my brain injury. One day I had a few hours alone in Grandma Maria's house and I wasn't feeling good on any level. That obsessive thought was always with me, but for some reason, on this particular day it felt unendurable. It was constantly at the front of my mind, making me feel worse than I already did. The only time I could ever escape this debilitating thought was when I slept. Whether I was speaking or silent, this thought hovered in my brain, just as the cloud once did. It's difficult to describe to anyone who hasn't been through this, but, even though I never stopped talking, I was always locked away somewhere in my mind with the accident Rosemary, this thought, and glimmers of the old Rosemary. The cloud had lifted, only to be replaced with this thought. Sounds like an even exchange, but the thought was much worse.

If I'd been capable of approaching this logically, that should have been all the proof I needed that no one could take my voice away. But it wasn't that easy. The thought refused to budge. I was forced to live in a prison cell of my own making, confined to the torture of my mind. The overwhelming torment of having absolutely no control over any part of the way I thought made life unbearable. The medication helped, but could never be enough.

And so, willing to do anything to make the torture go away even for a little while, I sat on my old bed with a recently refilled bottle of Xanax. I counted the pills slowly and had a bottle of water close by for when I summoned the courage to swallow them. Starring at the pills in a frazzled, confused state, there was still a little voice telling me not to do it. I thought about all the outcomes of taking that bottle of Xanax. My first thought was that at some point, I would just pass out and die. When I imagined that happening it scared me. Then I acknowledged that there was a possibility I could pass out and not die. When I thought about how I would feel afterward if they didn't kill me, that scared me, too. And then there was my mom, Grandma, and my sisters, not to mention all the pain I would be putting them through. Although I'd never believed in hell, it really bothered me that I didn't know where my soul would go if I died. As these thoughts rattled around in my head, it seemed that there was no way out.

After I'd sat there contemplating everything for a while, I put the pills back in the bottle.

Still rebellious, angry and tormented, I knew I wasn't done with the pills yet. I decided to take way more than I'd been prescribed, but hopefully not enough to die, which just shows that I wasn't thinking logically because I had no idea how many pills would kill me. What I wanted was to take enough to make my mind totally numb. Somehow—don't ask me how, because I don't know—I decided that the right number would be fourteen. Maybe it was because I was born on the fourteenth of September. Either way, that's how many I counted out, and that's how many I swallowed. For better or worse, it was done, and I felt good about it.

I never told my grandma what I had done. She acknowledged me a few times, but was busy doing her own things. She hadn't a clue what I was up to.

I started walking around outside. There was sunlight and a soft breeze. The temperature felt perfect. It was as though nothing abnormal was happening. But then I began to feel funny. Different. Slow. My stride and thought processes were impaired. If I had in fact taken the pills to numb my mind, it worked, because suddenly the thought was not right there like it always was. It was drowned out by this new feeling.

I remember walking back inside slowly through the side door of Grandma's kitchen, feeling so out of my mind, but this time in a totally different way. Grandma passed by me at some point, saying something that went in one ear and out the other. I walked around a bit more, then saw her again. She mentioned how I looked really tired and told me to go lie down and take a nap. Soon after that, I couldn't experience the conscious numbness anymore. I desperately needed to fall asleep. Walking back into my old bedroom, that's exactly what happened. I passed out as soon as I hit the sheets.

I slept and slept and slept. It was late at night when my grandma woke me up. She told me she'd better take me home because of the time. I had been sleeping for about five hours. When she took me home, I felt sick and shitty, and was still extremely tired. I went to bed again, and it took me days to recover. Lots of extra sleep. Throwing up. And lots of drowsiness. Nobody ever knew what I had done. They thought I was just under the weather. One cool thing was that during my recovery time, the thought didn't dominate me like it had before. But I knew I didn't want to take any Xanax for a while.

CHAPTER 24

Code Blue

Back at home, I still smoked cigarettes. Not a lot, just one or two a day. I'd take some from Sam's pack. He smoked Marlboro Light 100s. Gizmo and I would walk to the corner store once in a while to buy some Hot Cheetos, Laffy Taffy, and whatever else tickled my fancy at the time. I loved candy, and sweet candies were my favorite. Once I was home, I'd cut a lemon in half and dip every single Cheeto in that lemon until there was no lemon left. My hands would be stained bright red from the Cheeto and lemon juice mixture. It usually took a lot of handwashing and a few showers to get rid of it completely. Sometimes, I'd have a taste for chocolate bars, but I never cared for Tootsie Rolls, black licorice, Mounds bars, or any dark chocolate. I was a milk and white chocolate kind of girl.

My mom, being the manager at See's Candies, allowed us to have chocolate around the house sometimes, though not that often. Only on holidays and if we asked her. My favorite was the Bordeaux. I also loved the mini milk chocolate balls; they were the best to suck on. It was like having heaven in my mouth. People assumed we had chocolates at our house all the time, but it was never like that since Mom only got a twenty percent discount.

My facial scars were slowly healing. If I chose not to fix my limp, surgery was behind me. I didn't want to go through having to learn to walk all over again. Talk about no fun. The idea of not limping one day sounded glorious, but the biggest issue for me was the risk of going through surgery and rehab and still having the limp. Either way, I was facing another reconstructive surgery and a lengthy rehabilitation period. I didn't know for sure, but I was leaning toward not doing it.

During a walk with Gizmo to the corner store one afternoon, a passing car full of young guys slowed down in the middle of an intersection and yelled, "Learn how to walk, you stupid skinny bitch!"

As they drove away, laughing, tears rolled down my face. I felt rotten and wanted to get home as fast as my crippled leg could get me there. Luckily, Mom was home and I ran straight into her arms. After the crying subsided, I looked into her eyes and said, "Mommy, I want to have my last surgery."

My mind was surely set.

Mom made the appointment for me right away with Dr. Baldwin. I'll admit that it was comforting having such a dreamy doctor. I always thought my doctor looked just like Ben Affleck. And I wasn't the only one who thought he was a hot hunk. He was a medical doctor and a surgeon: looks, brains, and a sexy voice. I can't tell you how in love I was with him. Looking back, it was pure mental infatuation. Nonetheless, I felt safe in his care.

It's so funny because, brain injury and all, I still knew what I liked and wanted. He knew it, too, because I told him. One of his nurses rudely told me and Mom, after overhearing us talk about him, that he was happily married with two kids. She went on to say how beautiful and kind his wife was, too. She didn't like me getting any ideas. I mean, come on; it's not like he would've wanted my skinny, crazy ass anyway. At the time, I didn't care. Mom even said what a bitch that nurse was when she left the room. Cut the brain-injured girl a little slack, Mommy said!

I wasn't nervous when the day of my surgery arrived. Instead, I felt the excitement of getting to see Dr. Baldwin, and of getting this last surgery over with. I was also looking forward to getting my "happy shot" before being wheeled into the operating room. I loved feeling out of my mind, and this shot accomplished that. Mixed with my bruised brain, it also made me feel like laughing and singing.

A nurse came to prep me. The nurse knew how badly I wanted my happy shot since I kept raving about it. I wanted Mom to stay with me as long as they'd let her. She was able to go back and wait with me until it was time to go. Mom held my hand as they gave me the shot and it kicked in fast. I felt happy, loose, and totally giddy. I'm sure everything worked faster on me because I was such a lightweight. I had so much fun waiting there with Mom comforting me. I knew she couldn't stay much longer, but any nerves I had before were now gone, thanks to whatever drugs were in that shot. Feeling this way, I was okay with leaving her for a little while.

I felt spacey while the nurse wheeled me into a much bigger room and onto a more stable bed. Dr. Baldwin briefly greeted me, then I was left alone with a few other members of his team. They started putting IVs in both of my arms. Minutes later, a voice said they were about to give me some anesthesia and that I'd be passing out. Before I knew it, I was completely unconscious.

The next thing I remember was hellish. I could barely open my eyes. Everyone around me was running around frantically, and it felt like no one was paying any attention to me. Then a nurse came over and asked if I was feeling okay. I could barely nod my head. I felt like I'd been in a train wreck. Barely conscious, everything around me looked unreal, like I was in a horrible nightmare.

I was in the most excruciating pain I'd ever been in. Through slanted, dizzy eyes, I watched a concerned Dr. Baldwin speaking to someone in the corner of the room. I had no idea what was going on. The pain in my leg was getting worse. It felt like it had been chopped off. I tried to wave my arm to get his attention, but I couldn't.

After minutes of agony and despair, I gathered the strength to look down at my knee. It was all bloody and raw. I felt so sick, with the worst pain in the world vibrating through my entire body. Everyone looked as if a bomb had gone off. I knew something wasn't right.

Dr. Baldwin looked at me a couple of times, but he felt so far away. He never came to help me. Finally, at some point during this dreadful scene, a female nurse came to me and said something. I was so out of it that whatever was happening, was simply happening to me. I was able to speak a little and tell the nurse how much pain I was in. I recall her telling me they couldn't give me any more pain medicine, but I had no idea why.

A short time later, I was transferred to a rolling bed and taken to a small room. I was dying of thirst and felt worse than I'd ever felt in my life. The nurse told me that she was going to get my mom and I asked her to bring me some water, but she wouldn't give me water or pain medication even though I was begging for it.

I was more coherent, but still confused. When Mom walked into the room, she immediately hugged me. I told her how thirsty I was, along with the horrible pain I was in, and then she told me what had happened. I had died briefly on the operating table. My breathing had stopped, and I was given a shot of adrenaline to bring me back. She and Sam were so worried about me, and had witnessed the commotion from the waiting room.

It was all very difficult for me to make sense of. I wasn't feeling as happy and grateful as Mom did since I was still really confused, thirsty, and in a great deal of pain. I was told they couldn't give me any pain medicine or water for twenty-four hours. The adrenaline had burned through all the pain medicine that was previously in my body. To avoid any bad reactions, I had to wait for the adrenaline to wear off and there was nothing I could do but suffer through it. During those hours, it felt like my knee had been slaughtered. The pain was so raw, so rough, and so torturous. Nothing in my life had ever sucked more than this.

Mom stayed with me the whole night. She wasn't going to leave me alone. She told me that I couldn't have water or food for the same amount of time as the meds since my body couldn't handle it yet. But my mouth and throat were so dry. Even though the nurse denied us the first time we asked, when she came back to check on me, my mom begged her for anything they could do for me. The nurse brought me some ice chips to suck on. She made it clear that I was only to suck on them to get a bit of moisture in my mouth, and I had to promise not to swallow the water when they melted. She would bring another cup for me to spit in. Desperate for anything I could get, that was music to my ears.

Once she brought those two cups in the room, I serenely sucked on a few of the ice chips and they felt amazing. My mouth felt better, but my throat was still beyond dry. I ended up sneaking a little swallow. It was the tiniest amount. I couldn't wait until the morning.

Some time later, Mom called Sam to let him know she'd be staying the night. The nurse brought in a pillow and blanket for her. She shut off the light and we tried to get some sleep. The pain wouldn't let me sleep for a while, but eventually sleepiness took over. Mom slept on a chair in front of my bed. I'm sure I wasn't the only one uncomfortable that night.

The next morning, I was still in horrible pain. Mom asked the nurse for a pain pill right away, but she said we had to wait a few more hours. The nurse felt bad for me and kept coming back every thirty minutes or so, letting me know it would be soon. After hours of waiting, lunch was served with a side of Vicodin, water and orange juice. I knew I was in luck when the nurse walked in the room with a smile on her face. It was a very light meal; we were told I needed to eat light meals for the next week. But that Vicodin and glass of water were heaven-sent. I took it right away. Soon after lunch was finished, my pain diminished incredibly. I was finally at ease.

They wouldn't let me go home that day; I had to stay two more nights. Mom wanted to go home, but said she'd be back later. Even though I loved having her company, I had to let her go. I was feeling much better and slept most of the day away. Mom visited me later, but didn't need to stay the night.

On the third day, Dr. Baldwin came to see me and Mom. He checked up on me and gave us some instructions before I went home. Home had never sounded so sweet.

CHAPTER 25

My Healing Brain

Mom told the family the whole story at dinner, describing how she and Sam were in the waiting room during my surgery and heard someone yelling, "Code Blue! Code Blue!" It sounded so serious that she started to panic. When she asked the front desk what was going on, no one had any answers.

It turned out that another patient, one who was older than me, was also having surgery that day. When the older lady's kids asked a nurse if it was their mother, Mom overheard the nurse say that all the commotion was for a much younger lady. She knew then that something was terribly wrong. A short time later, a nurse came out to tell her they'd given me too much pain medicine during the surgery and that I had flatlined. She went on to say they had to give me adrenaline, but that I was going to be okay. After a long wait, they took Mom back to be with me.

Being handicapped with knee and leg issues again wasn't fun, but I made the most out of every day. I didn't expect the surgery to be so intense, but since I'd survived, I prayed it would all be worth it. *Dear universe, at least let my limp go away!*

After my first knee surgery, I had to leave it in a brace. But this time, it was different for some reason. I still had to wear a brace, but for eight hours a day, I had to put my leg on a device that kept my knee constantly moving. It sucked. I basically had to sleep on my back every night with my right leg up in the air on this gadget. Mom strapped my leg in securely so my knee wouldn't make any unnecessary movements. The first night I used it, my leg couldn't bend at all, so the dial was set to the slowest setting. Every week, my mom would raise the dial up a notch, just like the doctor ordered. This went on throughout my entire recovery process. It was uncomfortable in the beginning, but, like anything else, I got used to it.

I attended rehabilitation sessions three to four days a week again. Every night, I had Gizmo and a telephone to keep me company. I started calling Tele-Chat again and I'd talk to different guys while lying in bed. Vicodin was in my system to kill the pain, which I needed in order to feel as comfortable as possible. The phone conversations were all innocent. I loved to talk on the phone and in person, so it was a great way to pass the time.

Every morning when I woke up, I was in excruciating pain. I'd take a Vicodin first thing. I was so grateful for those pain pills; they really got me through a lot of suffering.

I was still thin, and it was so damn hard for me to get back to the weight I was at before the accident. I was down to seventy-six pounds when I left the hospital the very first time. I gained a little weight back by learning how to talk less and eat more at mealtimes, but never broke ninety. It seemed impossible for me to gain any more. I was eating all I could, and having lots of desserts before bedtime for good measure. I looked anorexic, but it wasn't my fault.

Mom was so great through everything. I still don't know how she did it. There was a movie called I *Don't Know How She Does It*, starring Sarah Jessica Parker, and when the previews first came out, my sisters and I said that movie was about our mom. Thanks to her, my recovery was going as well as it possibly could.

I was still friends with Dakota. Why I never learned to walk away from her, I don't know. She came over to my house one evening. Not just to visit, though—she had a proposition for me. It involved stealing another family member's car. Since I lived at home again, Dakota wanted to take my mom's car out while she was sleeping. She jocked this guy we went to high school with named Jack. He didn't live too far away, but any amount of driving was already too much for me. He lived next to my friend Donna, near the local In-N-Out Burger. It was two light signals and two stop signs away. A five-minute drive. We could've walked there, but she wanted to go in my mom's car and she wanted me to drive.

Obviously, I wasn't going to do that. I had a brain injury, I was in a brace, and my leg was almost immobile. Aside from that I hadn't forgotten what happened the last time Dakota persuaded me to steal a car. She got away with it, while I lost my grandmother's trust and came very close to being charged by the cops. Now, my driver's license was revoked, which I told Dakota. Usually one learns their lessons, but I didn't have a logical working mind then. She kept telling me everything would be fine, and I honestly believed her.

I went into Mom's purse, grabbed the keys, and drove away once she fell asleep. Dakota sat shotgun and we wheeled on over to Jack's pad.

We made it there safely and knocked on his back door. When Dakota told him I drove us over in my mom's car, Jack looked at me, then at my leg, and I could totally read the disbelief in his facial expression. We sat in his back room for a little while. His brother David went to junior high with my sister Alyssa. David's room was next door to Jack's. Jack asked if we wanted a bong rip and totally blazed us out.

After about fifteen minutes, David came in to say hi. Jack mentioned that I should go hang out with his brother in his room. Jack was cute, but I always thought his younger brother was cuter, so I wasn't opposed to it. I didn't know this was going to take place, but maybe that was their plan from the beginning. Even though the boys could see my physical injuries, they couldn't tell that anything was mentally wrong with me. It was exactly like the doctor had predicted; once the cloud was gone, the outer world would not know there was anything wrong inside my head. Physically, I had an injured leg, raised red scars on my forehead, a big red one under my right nostril, a long scar under my bottom lip from when I bit my lip off, and I was very skinny. Other than that I looked and seemed pretty much normal. Guess I still looked pretty anyway. I wore makeup, dressed in cute outfits, and Mom took me to get my hair and nails done on a regular basis. If David or Jack truly knew what was going on with me upstairs, I'm sure I would've been treated differently.

I went into David's bedroom and left Dakota and Jack alone. I knew what was going to happen. She'd wanted that guy for so long. She talked about it all the time.

David's room was completely dark except for the light from his TV. His bed and TV took up most of the floor space. We talked for a bit, sitting on that big freaking bed. I was high for sure. Soon, we started to make out. We kissed for a long time. He was cute, polite and innocent, so I didn't mind.

About thirty minutes later, we heard a knock on his door and Dakota's voice telling me it was time to go. We kissed a little more. I could feel we both didn't want it to end. When we heard the second knock we stopped. I got up, put my shoes on, and said goodbye. Still stoned and feeling good, I wondered if we'd ever talk or hook up again. We didn't.

While I drove us home, Dakota told me all about her and Jack's hookup. She asked me about David and what we did. When I finally got back to my house, I was happy to have made it home safe and sound. Everyone was still asleep when I walked through the back door. All the lights were off, and it looked exactly the same as when I left. I snuck Mom's keys back in her purse. When the morning arrived, she never knew a thing.

I loved when Mom would take me out with her somewhere; that was really my only opportunity to get out and see the world. Lots of times, though, when a girl would look at me, I'd immediately yell at them saying, "Stop looking at me, I was in a car accident!" For some reason, my mind would take me there, and I simply couldn't control those reactions.

While living at home, my life pretty much consisted of going shopping or out to eat once in a while, and sometimes visiting Grandma Maria and other relatives. Going to rehabilitation during the week was an outing, too, though it was less fun. Eating out afterward was always enjoyable. Spending time with my dog was always a daily delight, and I continued using the machine on my knee every night for eight hours.

Mentally, I was getting better, even with the odd extreme down times. Ups and downs, backs and forths, dips and loops: all of those tiny little cells inside my head were slowly trying to find their way home.

CHAPTER 26

Losing My Best Friend

I was living life the best way I knew how. At the same time, my lawyer was working hard on my behalf. I had to go to a deposition to meet the man who hit my car. He was an older man in his seventies. I knew I'd feel odd meeting him after everything I'd been through.

He ended up being such a nice guy. When he saw me, he looked very sad. I was never upset with him. I knew it was just an accident. Looking back, I feel sad for him, too. At the end of the deposition, he gave me a big hug and said that he was sorry. I said something to the effect of it being okay. I knew he didn't do it on purpose. It was all just an awful thing that happened to both of us. He wasn't hurt badly, but I'm sure he had pain in his heart as well as in his body. Besides the sadness in his eyes, I'm sure he had some psychological problems to contend with after the accident, but at least we were both alive. I always hoped that the person who hit me hadn't died or been severely injured. I thanked God for my sister's life. She was suffering with so much mental trauma from everything she saw that day, along with a bad case of whiplash, for which she had to wear a neck brace. I know all too well that the psychological part is the worst.

Back at home, Mom had been researching hypnotherapy. She'd heard great things about what it could do for stress, depression, anxiety, and many other problems. There was a local place that offered the treatment, so she booked me some sessions. I'd go once or twice a week for forty-five minutes at a time.

The place was owned by a couple. They seemed to be the only employees there, and I had a one-on-one session with either of them once a month. They'd talk to me and then hypnotize me. For my other visits, I would go into a private room, lay down on a firm bed, put on glasses that flashed a red light back and forth, and shut my eyes. They'd pick a cassette tape for me to listen to through headphones for the entire session. These tapes always featured soothing voices that would say wonderful, positive things.

> "You are such a wonderful, amazing person, with so many gifts to give to the world."
> "You are strong. You are healthy. You are one of a kind."
> "You love yourself and all people so much."
> "The world around you is a beautiful place with so many different opportunities."

Every time I walked out of there, I felt lighter and happier. I went there regularly for almost a year. Mom was really right about that place, and she saw so much improvement in my overall well-being. She told me that she'd noticed a positive change in me after the first visit, and it only got better from there.

But my positivity was about to face a huge challenge.

Most mornings I woke up kind of late to find Gizmo sleeping next to me on my pillow. One morning, he wasn't there. I called his name a few times but didn't see him. I looked out my bedroom window and saw Mom in her car in the driveway, about to take off somewhere.

I yelled out the window, "Where's Gizmo?" Grabbing my crutches, I made it out the front door and down the three steps to her car just as she was about to back away. "Mommy, where's Gizmo?"

She was flustered that day. "Oh gosh, I'm sorry. I forgot about him. He's on his leash in the backyard."

We didn't have a fence or gate in our backyard, so if he was left outside on his own, he'd run to the front yard, into the street, or wherever he pleased. We'd tie his leash to a pole by the back of the house so he could stay outside and take care of his business unsupervised, but usually for about fifteen minutes at a time.

It was hot that day and already after noon. I hobbled my way from the front yard to the back, where I knew he'd be. Turning the corner, I couldn't believe my eyes. He lay there, looking stiff as a board. His eyes were frozen open, lifeless.

"GIZMO! GIZMO!" I screamed over and over, but there was no response. He was dead. I screamed at the top of my lungs. People had to have heard me from blocks away. I hugged him and held his body in my arms, crying so hard that I became hysterical.

My mom rushed over. She'd heard my screams from down the street and immediately started crying her own eyes out. She kept telling me how sorry she was, pleading with me as uncontrollable tears ran down her face. As shocked and awful as I felt, I saw my mother's pain and despair clearly. I couldn't help but hug her and tell her that it was okay. I knew it was an accident.

That was one of the worst days of my life—Mom's, too. Gizmo was my best friend. I talked to him, laughed with him, and he was the only one who never judged me and understood me completely. He gave me so much support through all my struggles and pain. How could my black, wavy-haired dog—with his white goatee and thin red collar—who meant the world to me, be gone? He was angelic, beautiful, and a loving soul mate who slept by my side every single night. It was Gizmo who would listen to my happy laughter and comfort me when I cried. He knew both Rosemarys: the old Rosemary and the accident Rosemary. Having him by my side whenever I needed him always made things better. He was my Gizmo, my Gizzy, and now he wasn't there anymore. I was heartbroken.

I created a shrine to Gizmo with some photos, his red collar, and a few of his old toys. I also wrote a beautiful poem for him. Later, I found out that my sister Destiny had also written a brilliant poem about Gizmo. She really loved him, too. We all did.

My poor mom told me so many times how awful she felt. Over the coming months, Mom would often talk about wanting to get me a new dog. It felt too soon, but I had a brain injury and yearned for some doggie love, so I kept an open mind. Destiny had her outdoor, black and white cat Bailey. Mom had a cat that she adored, too, whom she'd named Truffles. He was a short-haired Siamese. Sam and Ryan's cat Kitty Koo Koo had already been gone for a while. I don't remember how he passed. We all had animals who we loved dearly at some time or other.

No dog could ever take the place of Gizmo, but I was lonely and wanted a companion. So, after some time had passed, I started to think about another dog. One afternoon, Mom took me to Petco in Covina where I totally fell in love with a cute dog that looked like a little stuffed teddy bear. He was a grey and white Lhasa Apso. With his cute little face and cuddly soft hair, we were warned that these dogs require lots of maintenance. The hair would eventually get long enough to cover his entire face and body; it could even get long enough to touch the floor. I imagined a werewolf the way the lady was describing it. But that's the dog I wanted. He wasn't cheap, either. The price tag on the window read "in the high $900s." That was way out of our price range, but the fact that my heart was set on it, coupled with my mother's overbearing guilt, meant I was going to get almost any dog I wanted.

That day we were only window-shopping. Nothing was set in stone, but I had a hunch I'd see that dog again. On my next birthday, I opened a big box and out popped that adorable teddy bear dog. He jumped out so happily and with all the energy in the world. So fluffy, so soft, so silky: he had that smooth touch, and his eyes were almost as sweet as Gizmo's. He kept jumping all over me and licking me, and we immediately started playing. I was happy. The dog was, too. I decided to name him Basil. Not because I was fond of the herb or anything, but because I remembered a guy I liked a long time ago named Basil. It seemed like the right name for this little pup.

Basil was a good dog. I came to care for him a lot, but Alyssa seemed to fall in love with him the hardest. As much as I tried, I still couldn't love him the way I'd loved Gizmo—not even close—but I loved him the best way I knew how, and we had great times together.

Meanwhile, I was finally done with my rehabilitation and with that machine. My knee was working well, I was walking again, and the limp was gone! I walked perfectly and felt like a million bucks.

I started talking to a new guy who was three years younger than me. Sometimes we would go out around town, but he always wanted to make out in public and I was way more private than that. I didn't understand why he wanted the whole world to see us making out. I would do it with him for a little while, but soon I became uncomfortable and ended up having to tell him.

During one of his visits at my house, my whole family suddenly realized that Basil wasn't around. We called his name but couldn't find him anywhere. That guy went outside to look for him. About ten minutes later, he came back holding Basil; he was dead in his arms. I started to cry. We all did. Basil had been hit by a car. He wasn't even a year old.

I vowed from that day forward that I would never own another dog as long as I lived. It was too painful. My heart simply couldn't handle it anymore.

CHAPTER 27

Violent Boyfriend

My mind was healing and I was still going through different stages on different levels—like in a Nintendo game, when after each level you upgrade and get closer to the finish line. When Mom delivered the news that my lawsuit was finally over, I felt like we could at last put that chapter behind us.

Everything had worked out in my favor. It wouldn't have if the other side were able to prove that there was no gas in my car, because then I would've been found at fault. But, the investigation concluded that there was a decent amount of gas in my car. Something that always amazed me and my mom was that my car insurance for the Prelude had only just kicked in the day of the accident. Keith had added me to his policy and offered to pay for it. It turned out I'd been unknowingly driving uninsured for two weeks before that.

I would get a monetary settlement, and my sister Destiny would also get one when she turned eighteen. My lawyer, Mom, and Sam all seemed satisfied. My stepdad had seriously been my savior in all of this. Not only had he rescued us all from poverty years before, but he was a supportive stepfather every step of the way in this ordeal. The great lawyer that helped us win the case was his company lawyer. Before and after my accident, Sam gave me his love and guidance. He was a hard worker, a provider, and finally I felt that protection that a good, honest male figure gives. For that, I will always be grateful.

Once my settlement was finalized and I was doing better mentally and physically, Mom and I both felt that I could start looking for an apartment or condo close by. After a little searching, we found a townhouse for rent in West Covina, about ten minutes away from our house. The price was reasonable, and the pictures looked great, so we made an appointment to do a walk-through. The place was beautiful: two stories, two bedrooms, two bathrooms, a decent size living room, a dining room, a laundry room, and a small kitchen. It even had a mini backyard with a fire pit and a two-car garage. The master bedroom had lots of closet space, the kind I'd always dreamed of. It was all perfect. The landlord was a nice middle-aged man named Bob. We kept in touch, and soon the place was mine.

After living there for about two weeks, I wanted an animal companion. Since it wasn't going to be a dog, the next logical option was a cat. I browsed my local penny-saver magazine and saw an orange and white Persian kitten, male, for $350. I picked up my new baby boy that same day and fell in love once again. He made me laugh and smile, and gave me so much joy. I named him Sage.

One day, while leaving a local 7-Eleven, I noticed this boy getting into his car. He gave me a big smile, then we started talking and exchanged phone numbers. Soon, that boy became my boyfriend. His name was Slater.

Slater seemed really nice. He was kind of short (around my height of five feet, six inches), and I thought he was cute. He started staying over at my condo all the time, and pretty soon moved in. My brain was at an interesting stage of recovery. It was better in the sense that I was more coherent and present, but what still wasn't right was my grip on life situations. I wasn't always well enough to make good decisions. That tormenting thought about losing my voice had slowly gotten quieter, but it still surfaced once in a while. I'd been a big weed smoker before my accident, but while I still smoked cigarettes and had a couple of beers here and there, I feared smoking weed again, thinking it might harm my healing brain.

Mom took care of all my bills for me. I got the money together, and she made sure they were all paid on time. Thanks to her, I built up an excellent credit score. I was making physical improvements, too. My facial scars were much less pronounced. I had a certain portion of my settlement money allocated for cosmetic surgery, but I knew I was never going to use it for that. I didn't want any more surgeries. My scars weren't fully healed, and I honestly didn't want to erase the physical memory of what I had been through. Those scars were a symbol of my journey—battle scars, if you will.

Mom wasn't exactly thrilled with the thought of a guy moving in with her daughter, especially when she didn't know if he was going to help pay rent—he didn't—but she wanted me to feel free and able to make my own choices, even if they weren't always good ones. She didn't want to be "that controlling mother type," as she put it. I liked having Slater there and he treated me well, except that he became obsessively jealous right away. Mom didn't know about that part, and I had no experience with that type of guy.

Slater didn't have a job, but he still had a source of income. He sold good weed and almost always had it on deck. Scared of doing anything else to mess with my brain, I passed up on opportunities to smoke with him for the first couple of months in our relationship. One day, during a talk with my sisters and friends about my concern, they all assured me that weed was harmless and, if anything, might help calm my mind. I finally decided to smoke it again.

It did calm me down, and had me taking less Xanax. Soon I was smoking it regularly. I didn't know if it was doing any damage to my healing brain, but I figured it couldn't be any worse than all the Xanax, Vicodin and Prozac I was already taking.

Slater's free pot ended up being the only good thing about him. His jealousy got much worse the longer we stayed together, and soon I saw a violent side to him. His temper was crazy and outrageous. He would throw and break things of mine when he was angry, like my cell phone, lamps, remote controls, figurines, and even pipes. Anything within his reach, really. He'd even rip up meaningful photographs of mine. Then he got physically abusive with me. Socking me a lot was his thing. Before long, I had different bruises on various parts of my body.

He gave me a black eye once, and a few times he pushed me so hard that I fell down. I never told any of my family or friends. I don't know why; I was very insecure and just dealt with it. If the bruises looked too bad, I'd wear long sleeves and cover them up. If one was visible and I couldn't hide it, I'd make up a story about how I got it.

Things got worse, and I became frightened. One time he called me drunk from a friend's house in Hacienda Heights and told me to come pick him up. When we drove away, he started screaming at me. Before I knew it, he was socking my right arm over and over. He did that all the way home. When I parked in the garage, my arm hurt so damn badly. Still sitting in the car with me, he started kicking my windshield as hard as he could, until he ended up shattering the glass on the passenger side. It was awful, and I had no idea why any of this was happening.

The next day, my entire right arm was black and blue and it hurt tremendously. I avoided my family for a week or so because of the bruises, which looked even worse as the days went by. I was scared of how far Slater would go to hurt me, and I didn't want to keep this violence a secret any longer. My mom and Sam had recently separated due to marital issues. She'd had her own place for about a year, and I didn't want to bother her with my problems. To be honest, I simply wasn't thinking clearly. Eventually, I went over to her new little condo in Covina. When I got there, Mom was at work, but both of my sisters were there with my brother. I sat on the couch and listened to their conversation. I wasn't going to say anything until there was a break. When the break came, I took off my sweater and they all looked at my arm in astonishment.

They all asked what happened, and I clearly remember my brother asking, "Who the hell did that to you?"

He was really upset, and when I told him and my sisters what happened, they were all mad. I'd never seen Ryan so pissed off in all my life. It felt good to get it off my chest, though. My brother wanted to kick Slater's ass, and they all told me I had to leave him—end of story. My brain wasn't that smart yet, but it, and my heart knew that was the right thing to do. I was scared, though. Slater had told me to keep my arms covered and to never show anyone. I agreed, so he had no clue that I did. I'd planned to confess to my family. I honestly feared for my life. I felt he was capable of anything. Plus, I'd been supporting him the whole time we'd been together; he wasn't going to like the idea of not being able to live off me for free anymore. But no matter what, I was set on leaving him.

He didn't like it one bit when I told him. He was angry. I didn't feel right about staying in the condo with him, nor did my family. Mom told me that I needed to move in with her until he was gone. We gave him a month to find a place of his own.

While I was packing the night before I left to stay with Mom, Slater and I got in a big fight. It was the worst one yet, and he went ballistic on me. He was screaming at me and then things started to get physical. I got really scared and ran upstairs to my bedroom, but he chased me. I tried to close the door and lock it, but I didn't get the chance. He pushed me to the floor, yelled at me, then grabbed my neck and started choking me. I couldn't breathe. He knew, but he didn't seem to care. I stared at him in horror and he stared back at me with such angry eyes. I thought I was going to die. Then he let go of my neck.

I gasped for air, coughing and trying my hardest to get my breath back. He looked at me barely sitting up on the floor with disgust on his face. I couldn't get up right away. I kept weeping and he kept yelling. I had to listen to every word of it. Finally, when I gained the strength to pick myself up, I started to run down the stairs. I got halfway down, but then he pushed me the rest of the way. I lost control once his hand touched my back and crashed into the wall. It hurt, but I was okay.

At some point, I grabbed my phone, ran outside and called someone to come pick me up. The rest of the night is a blur to me. I was just thankful to be alive. My cat Sage and I moved into mom's house immediately after that. Slater wanted me to leave Sage with him, but there was no way in hell that was going to happen. The next day, I went back to the condo with Mom to grab some of my things. Slater knew I was coming, so he stayed away.

I knew he would probably steal whatever he wanted from me, but I didn't care. I was simply happy to be alive and I couldn't wait for him to be gone. About a week later, Slater called to tell me that his twin sister desperately needed a place to stay for a little while and that he was finding it difficult to find a place for himself. To keep things peaceful, I let them both stay there. I told him I'd given the landlord a thirty-day notice, so he had to be gone in three weeks, and that I still needed time to move my stuff out. He agreed. The truth is, I never gave my notice, but Mom and I knew that would be the only way to get him out. I was paying the rent the entire time, but that was small potatoes. His sister was the same size as me, but a hardcore *chola* bitch. I didn't like the idea of her living there with all of my clothes and belongings. I was sure there was a lot of nice stuff there she'd have liked to take, but that was how things had to be.

One day, while I was home alone at Mom's, the doorbell rang. I looked through the peephole and saw it was Slater. Not wanting to let him in, I went to the window and opened the blinds, then asked him what he wanted. Sage jumped on the windowsill as I was talking. Slater told me to open the door so we could talk. He was getting mad and I was scared. I told him if he didn't leave, I'd call the cops. That made him nervous, so he said he'd leave. Right before he did, he took a good long look at my cat and said, "I'm gonna kill Sage!"

He left after that, then I grabbed Sage and held him tightly for a while.

When the month was up, they had found a place and left mine. Slater told me that his sister wanted to thank me for letting her stay there. He assumed I'd found another place like I told him I would. After a week of them being gone, I felt safe enough to move back home. I did fear Slater would maybe try to find me, or visit the condo again to see if I was lying about moving out. Fortunately, he never did. I imagined that his sister must have had some kind of talk with him because she was so grateful for what I did for her and her brother. Whatever the reason, I was extremely happy and relieved to have him out of my life.

CHAPTER 28

Drugs, Alcohol and Partying

Having my condo to myself, and with no guy around to take advantage of me, control me, or abuse me, made me feel like I was truly free again. And at this point in my life, I was well enough to want to go out and party sometimes. The friends I went out with knew my situation, so they understood that I wasn't the old Rosemary they'd once known. I was a bit wild and crazy before my accident, but afterward I'd taken it to a different extreme. My new attributes only added fuel to my fire. The fire burning within me was a wildfire that needed serious extinguishing.

I'd left all common sense behind, and I didn't care. I did whatever I pleased, even if the situations seemed risky and dangerous. I trusted everybody I met, and never thought anyone or any situation could harm me, or even gave anything a second thought. If one of my friends was down for something, whatever it was, I was down for it, too. Except for when my mind took me into a deeply obsessive, debilitating place, nothing scared me. I still had those episodes sometimes, but getting out and exploring the world around me excited me enough to overpower those thoughts. Getting wasted probably helped diminish them, too. I often went to bars and clubs, and participated in lots of self-medicating. I was able to handle substances well, and not being in my normal state of mind felt good.

My drugs of choice were Vicodin, Xanax, alcohol, weed and cigarettes. Just one of them, or—even better—mixing them together, felt fantastic. I never worried or even thought of the possibility of anything bad happening to me. To be honest, during this stage and with the state of mind I was in, I don't think I even knew it was possible. I felt untouchable, and every time I went to a bar, a club, or someone's house to drink, I'd already have Xanax and/or Vicodin in my system. My favorite drink was Red Bull and Grey Goose vodka. All other vodkas tasted like rubbing alcohol to me, especially Smirnoff. So that's how I rolled. Weed and cigarettes were always part of the scene no matter what.

I went out with Gizelle or Dakota most of the time, but much more so with Gizelle. She loved the Newport Beach scene, and for a while we went there every weekend. We often hit up three clubs in that area: Sutra, Club Vegas, and The Shark Club. The Shark Club was the one we seemed to go to the most.

I remember two nights in particular as the craziest. The first happened at the Shark Club: a big club in Newport that was always jam-packed. Gizelle was friendly with Jeremy Jackson, an actor who worked there and helped promote the club. Jeremy was famous for playing Hobie on the TV show *Baywatch*. That might have been the reason we went to that club so often. The night I'm thinking of, Gizelle and I were both doing our own thing. I was a lightweight, but I always ordered double shots in my drinks and had two or three of them. At some point in the evening, I climbed onto a platform above the dance floor. Girls danced on this bar thing, while the rest of the club below looked up. I ended up dancing alongside a blond Russian chick who was as drunk as I was.

As we danced, we kept looking at each other, smiling, flirting. Then two guys below yelled up at us to kiss, so we did. It turned out one of the guys was her boyfriend. When she eventually got down, I followed her. Her boyfriend told me I should come home with them. I had no idea where Gizelle was. It was almost one in the morning, so I left those people and went off on my own to find her, but I found my way to the VIP room and its bar instead. I don't remember how, but somehow I got ahold of a wristband that allowed me in there. I asked some guy inside to buy me a drink. When he ordered it, a security guard told me that I was already too drunk and that if I had another he'd have to kick me out. I agreed, but I wasn't serious at all.

The song "Toxic" by Britney Spears started playing. There was a much smaller stage in there with a few girls dancing on it. One of them told me to join them. I was wasted as some girl helped me up. Meanwhile, the bouncer kept a close eye on me. I guess he was really serious about me not getting another drink, and I was obviously out of control. For whatever reason, I totally disregarded him, and after the song was over, I got down off the stage and headed to the bar. I asked another random guy if he could please buy me a Red Bull and vodka. Not giving a mad hoot about that bouncer, I started drinking it. The bouncer came over and told me to put the drink down and leave the club.

The next thing I knew, I was running out of the VIP room and back into the crowded club, drink in hand, with the bouncer chasing me. I kept running as fast as I could. I don't know where my mind was, but I told myself it was a game. It must've been entertaining for everyone else watching this go down. When the bouncer finally caught up with me, he grabbed my drink and escorted me outside. I remember he was so pissed off.

I sat alone on the curb for a while, with people walking by and looking at me. Then I saw Gizelle. She came over and told me she'd been looking for me everywhere and saw me running from the bouncer. When she spoke with him afterward, he told her he'd kicked me out. She was happy to have found me, and asked me to wait there while she went back inside to say goodbye to Jeremy. Still drunk as heck, I told her I'd wait. About ten minutes later, I saw the boyfriend of that Russian girl I was making out with earlier. Then I saw her and their friend. The boyfriend was cute and had light brown hair; the friend had dark hair and wore glasses. That's all I remember about them. The friend walked over to me and asked if I was okay, if I was stranded and needed a ride, and if so, he assured me I could go with them. I agreed to tag along, got up to leave with them, and forgot all about Gizelle.

As we were all walking away, Gizelle ran over and told me not to leave with them. But I didn't listen. Once we got in the car, I was told they were too drunk to drive me all the way home. The friend said he'd drive me home in the morning. They took me back to their apartment in Newport Beach. Once we were inside, the couple went straight to their bedroom without even acknowledging me. The friend got me a blanket and said I could sleep on the couch. He took the love seat. We chatted for a little bit, then he turned off the lights and we fell asleep. Luckily, this guy was nice. If he hadn't been, he could have so easily taken advantage of me.

When I woke up, I was safe and sound on the couch, and he was still sleeping on the love seat. It was around seven in the morning. I just lay there, waiting for the guy to wake up. About half an hour later he did, then asked me if I wanted to go home. I never did see that Russian girl or her boyfriend again. He dropped me off at home unharmed. I was so lucky everything worked out in my favor, and yet I didn't even realize it at the time. I was simply too trusting of strangers.

The second memory was this time at Sutra. The club's atmosphere was classy and seductive. It was a much more elegant looking place with beautiful gold, pink and purple ambient lighting. Sutra didn't have elevated public dance floors, but girls that were hired to dance up above everybody else. These women dressed alike and performed exotic, sexy dance routines. They also had poles to work with.

There was a guy named Brandon that we saw a lot at the different clubs we went to. We had danced together before, but that was it. We never exchanged phone numbers, kissed, or anything. I always felt that I wouldn't have minded if we had; he was really cute. When Gizelle and I ran into him again, we talked briefly, then parted ways. Closing time came around, and we ran into him again outside. He asked us where we were headed. Gizelle was never drunk and was always our designated driver. She usually just had one beer at the beginning of the night, sometimes another later. I, on the other hand, always had a few drinks. Brandon didn't live far from the club and said that if we still felt like chilling, we should go over to his place. We were still wide awake, and agreed we'd stop by for a little bit. We followed him home. He told us where to park, and then he walked us up to his apartment on the second floor. There was a big bed, a little refrigerator, a couple of chairs, and a big stripper pole right in the middle of the floor. He grabbed us all a beer and we sat around chatting.

After about fifteen minutes of talking, we somehow ended up on the subject of roofies. I think I might have mentioned how I never leave my drink unattended. Brandon started telling us how he had some roofies, and that it wasn't as bad as we thought. He got up and took out a tall plastic arrowhead water bottle full of the liquid. He told us that you only needed a tiny amount for it to work. Any more could be dangerous. We asked him how it felt and if he ever took it. He said he took it a lot, but only a cap full. We told him to take it in front of us, so he did. He made this disgusted face right after and said it tasted horrible. Then he told us to take some, too. We were a little hesitant, but we were both so wild back then that we ended up going for it. Gizelle took it first, then me. It had the worst taste my taste buds had ever encountered.

After about twenty minutes, these odd sensations started to wash over me. We started laughing uncontrollably. Then we got up and started dancing on his stripper pole. We didn't strip, though. Everything looked all wobbly; it was like moving in slow motion.

We continued drinking our beers, but couldn't finish them. As time progressed, the feeling started wearing off, but I still felt dazed and confused. Like the high from smoking weed times a hundred, then mixed with something else. Gizelle must have felt similarly, but she was ready to leave. She wasn't drunk to begin with like me, and hadn't smoked any weed, so that was probably why she felt she could drive. Brandon wanted me to stay, so I did. All I know is I thought he was really cute, and I was sleepy. We lay down on his bed, kissing, and then I must have passed out. The next thing I remember is some girl coming into his room in the morning to wake him up. She saw me in his bed and looked really mad.

I had an awful headache and smoked weed right away to counteract the shitty way I was feeling. He hopped out of bed and put on a shirt. My clothes were still on. I remember kissing him, but that was all. He took me home. It was a crazy-ass night. I'll never know what exactly was in that liquid, but I'll never willingly drink such a thing again.

Dakota and I still hung out sometimes, but we'd usually stick to TGI Fridays, B.J.'s, or dive bars in the neighborhood. One night, Gizelle, Dakota and I made plans to go to an 18-and-over club in

Anaheim called The Boogie. We had all been there plenty of times together as teenagers and loved it. It was always crowded and so happening. The only difference now was that we were all twenty-one. Dakota and Gizelle came over to my house to get ready an hour before we planned on leaving.

One minute, we were all putting on makeup and doing our hair. The next, I woke up in a hospital room. As I opened my eyes, wondering what on earth was going on, I looked around and saw Mom, Gizelle and Dakota. I asked if I'd been in another car accident.

"No, honey, you had a seizure," said Mom.

I simply did not understand. This had never happened to me before. All I knew was that being in the hospital again really sucked. I was so tired of hospitals. Dakota and Gizelle only stayed for a little while longer after I woke up, then they left.

I cooled down on going out for a while. The DMV took my driver's license away because of the seizure. I guess they were concerned I'd have another one behind the wheel. It made sense, but I wondered what caused this to happen to me. The only way I'd get my license back would be if a neurologist wrote a letter stating that he felt confident I wouldn't have another seizure. I didn't know how everything was going to work out. I just wished, imagined and prayed everything would go in my favor. To determine my fate as a driver, I had to have some tests done: a CAT scan and whatever else the doctor ordered.

Mom thought that it could possibly have had something to do with the hypnosis sessions. I had already been going for a year, and even had my own tapes, headphones, and a pair of those glasses with pulsing red lights to use at home. Mom called the hypnosis center to ask if there could be any connection, and it turned out that the flashing glasses and my seizure could have been related. It was a small possibility, but it was there. Only one percent of people who used those flashing glasses suffered from seizures. My mom was told that, if there was a problem, it would have happened during the session while the glasses were on. When I heard that, I thought that maybe in my particular case, I'd had a delayed reaction because of my brain injury. So far, that didn't seem to be enough to put the two together as the probable cause.

I eventually took all the tests we needed for a proper diagnosis. When the results were in, the neurologist said he could see no reason why I would have another seizure. He said it was a fluke, and believed it was caused by old scar tissue in my brain from the car accident. He assured us that he strongly believed it wouldn't happen again.

This was the best news we could have received. It meant I was going to be okay to drive again. He wrote to the DMV on my behalf, and I was sure I'd get my license back. I was ecstatic.

CHAPTER 29

Stoned and Stupid

My condo became sort of like "the party house," or "the kick back pad." It was certainly a chill place. People could come over and relax with no worries. We even had a couple of major parties. At one of them, we actually charged admission at the door. It's so hilarious thinking back on it now.

Mom had asked if my sister Destiny could live at the condo with me for a while. I was totally cool with it. The thing I appreciated most of all about that arrangement was that Destiny could calm my mind down with her constant reassurance. She has always been such a precious jewel to me. Having her there when my mind went haywire with a disturbing thought or idea gave me immediate clarification and reassuring love.

My mind still got stuck on troubling thoughts or ideas. Even when I knew the logical answer in my heart, my mind would screw me over and betray me with lies. It was like I could feel my brain cells not communicating properly. It was hard to deal with, and having my sister there to answer any crippling questions was wonderful. I could ask her all these dumb questions, and I wouldn't have to feel stupid. I couldn't do that with my friends. My family would see the different changes in me, but of course could never truly know what it felt like. I'd share things with them, and they'd see the pain it caused me.

For some reason, at that time I really wanted a pet fish. Mom and I went to a pet store to buy a tank for the condo, and I ended up coming home with three little fishes. Each week, one died. I had no clue why this was happening. I never thought in a million years that one fish would kill another. The guy who sold them to us said they were fine to live together in the same tank. What they didn't tell me was that these types of fish were cannibalistic fish eaters. After about a year, I found this out for myself. One fish outlived the rest. I thought he was a special fish, since he was the only survivor. I named him Cichlid after someone told me that was what kind of fish he was. I loved him dearly.

Destiny brought her tabby cat Marley to live with us, and I had my cat Sage, plus a new one that my Grandma Lucy had rescued in the high desert. She was a Siamese Himalayan, and I named her Jasmine. Jasmine started acting funny toward Destiny, and for some reason kept peeing on her sheets. We tried to keep her out of Destiny's bedroom by always making sure the door was closed. But we forgot a few times, and that's when Jasmine would strike again. I'd hear a sudden scream and Destiny yelling, "Jasmine peed on my bed again!" I couldn't help but laugh, even though I knew she was so annoyed.

Aside from that, we all got along well. It was awesome that my sister smoked weed, too.

Destiny's friends would often come over to the condo. She had three close guy friends— Kyle, Richie and Jake—but she wasn't dating any of them. Destiny was just chill like that. She also had two good girlfriends—Daisy and Ashley. The boys were all big weed smokers like us, but Daisy and Ashley, not so much. My brother Ryan also hung out with them, as they were all the same age. Everyone loved my cat Sage, and he really enjoyed the weed smoke. I had a pretty round glass table, and every time we'd gather around it to smoke weed out of my Jerome Baker bong, Sage would jump up on the table and flop down right in the middle to happily breathe in all the smoky air. He was such a cute and funny cat.

One fun and memorable night involved a sleepover at our pad with Alyssa and our cousin Michael. The night was filled with fun, love, joy, laughter, *Seinfeld*, and of course, smoking pot. We all loved to smoke, but Destiny and I loved it the most.

We all got super high, and as the night wore on, my sisters fell asleep in sleeping bags on the living room floor. Michael and I were still awake and I wanted to smoke more weed. But when I went to try and do just that, I realized the lighter had stopped working. I needed one last hit to complete my nightly regimen. Not having a working lighter in the house made me want that hit even more.

Frustrated and eager, I came up with this alternative plan of rolling a paper towel as tightly as possible and using it like a wick. I figured I'd light it off the burner on my stovetop, then apply the burning end to the bowl, take my hit, put it in the kitchen sink, and turn on the water to extinguish it.

Well, my plan backfired. Quite literally, too. The paper towel burned too quickly. As I put the pipe to my lips, I felt the searing heat of open flames brush against my hand. I screamed and threw the burning paper towel onto the living room carpet, which immediately caught fire. Michael and I panicked, then stupidly tried putting out the flames with handfuls of water from the kitchen sink. It wasn't enough, so the fire started to spread. Alyssa and Destiny woke up when they heard our screams and started freaking out. But they were smarter than us and got cups and bowls of water to extinguish the small fire. If they hadn't helped, we might have had to call the fire department.

After the fire was out, there was a big, dark burn the size of a suitcase on the rug. Mom had bought me a new cleaner called OxiClean. It worked quite well, but I didn't think it would work on a burn mark. I was pretty sure it wasn't made for that. But Alyssa must have still been stoned, because her first reaction after this ordeal was to yell, "Oh my God. Oh my God, get the OxiClean. Get the OxiClean!"

She grabbed it and poured the whole bottle out over that large burn mark. She said to let it sit for a while, so we did. Then, when she felt it was time to try scrubbing it away, she gave it a shot. We all helped a little, but she was the one who did the most; she scrubbed her little heart out. But it didn't help at all. I knew there was going to be big trouble with my landlord. I'd have to come up with a story to explain to both him and my mom how the burn got there.

I never got to smoke my last hit that night.

One Friday night, when Gizelle asked me if I wanted to go to Newport Beach with her, I realized we hadn't been to a club in a while, so I said I was up for it. Destiny and Ryan asked if they could have a little kick back while I was out. It was just going to be their close friends coming over, maybe a few others. By the time I finished getting ready to go out, most of their friends were already there, smoking weed and drinking beers—the usual.

Gizelle picked me up, and as we were backing out of the driveway, I saw the front door open and my beloved cat Sage roaming free right in front of the condo. Ryan was outside smoking a cigarette with one of his friends. I could tell he was already faded, but I yelled out the car window to let him know Sage was outside. I told him to put the cat in my room and shut the door. He slurred back that he would, gazing at me through bloodshot eyes. Why I trusted him, why I didn't get out of the car and pick Sage up myself is beyond me. It's something I'll regret deeply for the rest of my life.

When we were done for the night, Gizelle drove me home. I

opened the front door and looked around my messy house. Beer bottles were everywhere, trash was scattered all around. Ryan and two friends were passed out on the couch.

I looked for Sage right away. Every time I came home, Sage was there to greet me. That didn't happen this time. I didn't see him in the living room, so I assumed he was upstairs in my room. But he wasn't there, either. I searched every part of the house but couldn't find my baby. Ryan was barely responsive when I shook him awake and asked him where Sage was. He said he didn't know. I asked him if he brought him back inside the house like I'd asked, and he didn't seem to know what I was talking about. I got the feeling he never bothered to get him for me. I went outside, calling Sage's name, hoping he'd come running over to me. I felt so stupid and sad. I was going to have to sleep alone now.

"I'm sorry, Sage. I hope you are not too cold, hungry, hurt or thirsty. Please God, let me find my Sage tomorrow," I prayed.

In the morning, I hounded my brother about it. He played stupid. He'd been faded as hell, so I couldn't blame him. If only I'd rescued Sage and locked him safely in my room, I might've still had him.

I made posters with a photo of Sage and the offer of a $500 reward, but it was no good. Sage was never found. I'm so sorry, Sage. I will love and miss you forever.

CHAPTER 30

New Boyfriend and a Wilder Me

Every day, I thought about the ten years I had to get through before my brain would be fully healed. By the time 2006 rolled around, Destiny was eighteen and would finally receive her settlement lump sum of cash. She planned to move out and get her own place.

To go along with the new apartment, she had a new boyfriend named Ronny, who happened to be the son of our mom's best friend Dena. They used to waitress together at The Lobby, so Mom knew Dena even before she met Sam. They always shared a very close relationship.

I found myself living alone again, and before long I met a new guy of my own. His name was Lathan, and we met in Long Beach. We talked, we laughed, and we hit it off instantly. He didn't have a car, and he was living in a motel room out there that his mother paid for. By this time, I'd gotten my driver's license back and was able to drive down to Long Beach to chill with him sometimes.

Lathan was cute and nice, and he was only a year younger than me. We'd go out to eat and do fun things around the beach.

We talked on the phone every day. He wanted to know where I lived, so soon I brought him over to see my condo. It must have been convenient for him to meet a girl that liked him and had her own place, given that he was living off his mother in a motel with no job.

To be honest, I was still very insecure. I liked this guy in a big way, and felt he'd like me more if he found out how much money I had, and saw how I was able to afford such a nice place all on my own. I decided to tell him everything about my settlement. I felt that by telling him about everything I had, I could lock him down for myself.

And I did. We became a couple right away. I let him move in with me just a week after that. The relationship was definitely moving fast. I didn't grasp the concept of what I could and probably was creating: another man dependent on me. I was paying all the bills again, and since I was the only one with a car, I bought all the groceries, gas, dinners, etc. Having someone live off me was an easy, vicious cycle to fall into.

And once you allow it, dependent people expect that treatment all of the time. For whatever reason, taking care of another person without asking for anything in return can make you a weak, vulnerable enabler who is often taken advantage of. In the beginning, it might not seem so bad, and maybe for some people it never ends up being a bother. But most eventually reach their breaking point. It's a sickness.

I understand that now, but for some reason I didn't mind being taken advantage of then. It probably had more to do with my insecurity and not wanting to be alone. I liked having someone there, even if I had to pay for it.

My rescued cat Jasmine lived with Mom by then, Marley was with Destiny in her new home, and my cat Sage was still missing. I really missed animal love. I loved cats so much, and so did Lathan. One day, we went to the local Humane Society shelter in Baldwin Park and adopted two kittens. Lathan chose a black male with one little white patch and named him Rhino. I chose a multi-colored female that was mainly white and grey with blue eyes; I named her Halo.

I ended up having one more big party after my landlord specifically warned me to never have another. It got so big that the cops were called, so he found out. He wanted me to leave, which was totally understandable. I was going to have to find a new place to live.

Lathan and I had been to a bar in Covina called Clancy's a few times, and we really liked it. It had three pool tables, five dartboards, a cool bar area, nice people, and they allowed smoking inside. We were both smokers, so this was an ideal place to go. There happened to be apartments for rent almost right across the street, so we ended up moving into the neighborhood. Living so close by meant we became regulars. Most of the time we walked there. We got to know all the people really well, including the bartenders.

The most interesting thing occurred one night while we were at the bar. I had mentioned my dad's name to a bartender. Some man overheard me and said, "Raymond's your dad?" I nodded and he began telling me a few little stories about their past gangster friendship, including how it ended. I just listened in astonishment. He told me that my dad was the best looking *cholo* and how they all used to call him "the Brooke Shields" of the gang! I thought that was so cool and funny. After that night, I saw that guy a few more times at the bar or while he was out riding his bike. We always stayed friendly after that meeting.

Destiny had to move out of her apartment, so we happily agreed to take her cat Marley, along with Peaches. Peaches was a sweet homeless cat that magically appeared on my mom's front porch one afternoon. I fell in love with that orange and white cat, so he became part of my family. We now had a total of four cats living with us.

We smoked weed throughout the day, along with cigarettes, and did whatever around the house. We went to Clancy's about four nights a week, and chilled out with our television, old-school Nintendo, and the cats. There was a Jack in the Box drive-thru right by the new apartment, as well as a McDonald's. We ate there at least a few nights a week, basically living on fast food. I don't think either of us ever cooked a meal there unless the microwave was involved.

Every night at the bar, I ordered my usual double Grey Goose and Red Bull over ice, and I'd bring my pot with me to smoke outside after I finished my first drink. There was this perfectly secluded place to smoke, too. Back then, I was all about living for the moment, going out, getting faded, and having fun. I didn't worry at all. I was this fearless, rebellious, careless party girl. I'd have to say that I was in stage twenty of my brain injury's recovery process. I really didn't care much about anything or anyone. Not even myself. Oblivious to reality, I lived every moment as if it would last forever. I was never sober. Actually, my idea of sobriety was making sure there was weed in my system. The days I spent without it were awful. I didn't feel normal on any level, but I didn't care about the bad choices I was making. It was like I was able to block out the world around me. I didn't like the real world; I liked just being in my own dimension.

In this stage of my life, I felt like acting out, not giving a damn, and being beyond irresponsible. I was taking my life for granted. Without any goals or aspirations, I partied like there was no tomorrow and got lost in a very strange version of reality. It was simply about having fun, getting high, drinking, shooting pool, playing darts, and talking to new people.

Part of me was angry. I think it was because, for a long time, I'd felt like such an outcast in my family. I hadn't truly fit in with them for years. Ever since my accident, my relationships with them had diminished. To me, anyway. My strongest familial bond was with my sister Destiny. I felt a closeness with her that didn't exist with the others. When I say my ties with them had diminished, I mean in the sense that I always felt distant in our intellectual relationships. No matter how many years passed, I still felt like "the accident girl." Even if I was having an intelligent conversation with one of them, I felt like I was never taken seriously. I was stupid, crazy Rosemary who was in a bad car accident, and whose brain got messed up. And I had been screwed up for so long, it was going to take a lot of healing for them to see me differently. I knew I still had a lot more healing to do. At the same time, I also knew how much they loved me.

Even though I'd come a long way, I still had a few more years left to reach that decade mark. It's funny how fixated I was on reaching the ten-year mark. As if that was when the magic spell would break.

I was an adult, but I sure as hell didn't feel like one. Instead, I felt like an out of control high school girl with money to live on. My money was never spent on anything smart or worthwhile. I bought a light blue Volkswagen Beetle turbo convertible. It was the second car I'd owned since my accident; the first was a 2002 white Cabrio convertible that was wrecked when I made an illegal U-turn and hit another car. I was sober from a legal standpoint, but my state of mind caused me to flee the accident scene, laughing. Gizelle was with me and told me to go back, but I had no intention of that until my sister Destiny frantically called my cell, asking if I'd been in an accident.

It turned out her friend Maggie lived in the apartment complex right next to where the accident took place. All her friends knew what my car looked like since I often picked Destiny up from school. My decked-out, black and white, zebra print convertible was hard to miss. Destiny said I needed to go back because the cops and paramedics were there, and Maggie said they were all talking about me and my car.

Thank God for that phone call. If it wasn't for that, I wouldn't have gone back, and I would have been in major trouble.

I drove back to the scene of the crash. It was on the same street as Covina High School, just a couple of stoplights away. Once I arrived, a police officer came over to me. I apologized as he started questioning me. The people whose car I'd hit were looking at me, and they seemed all shaken up. The officer took my information and got my side of the story. When I asked if I was in trouble, he explained that I would have been if I hadn't come back. Then he described what would probably happen with my insurance company. He assured me everything was going to be okay because the other people didn't complain about being hurt. After I returned, they tried to change their story, to say they were in pain, but the report had already been taken and the officer told them he couldn't change it. Lucky me—again. My car never ran the same after that. Eventually, I had to get rid of it, and that's when I got my new blue Beetle.

After owning it for about two years, I drove it one night from Clancy's to another bar called Elvie's. It was right next door to the first Jack in the Box I ever worked at, and had the privilege of being the hometown bar to all the Covina heads. After about two hours, I decided to drive back to Clancy's. When I pulled out of the parking lot, I heard sirens and almost immediately got pulled over. I was drunk, and hadn't even made it a block before being caught.

A male police officer tapped on my window and asked me for my license and registration. Then he asked me if I'd been drinking. I told the truth, because even if I'd chosen to lie that night, he would have known. There was no way to hide how faded I was.

When I got drunk back then, I could act crazy. The officer ended up having to forcibly remove me from my car. I kicked and screamed like a little girl, yelling at the top of my lungs, "Help! Help! You're hurting me! You can't hurt me like this!"

Eventually, I was handcuffed and placed in the back of the police car. They took me to the local police station to spend the night behind bars. I was told my car would be towed. When they released me in the morning, I felt sick and bummed out. I was scared, too. I couldn't believe what had happened. As I walked alone to the Azusa bus stop to catch a ride home, I knew I wasn't headed down the right path in life.

CHAPTER 31

Reckless Rosemary

Now I had a DUI on my record, and I lost my license for three months. I had to attend two-hour classes once a week, and complete seven AA meetings within a certain timeframe. The DUI program cost me $64 a month, and court fees were another couple thousand dollars. I deserved these consequences, though. Things could've been much worse, and thankfully no one got hurt.

With my car taken away, I had to take buses everywhere, so the only places I really went to were local spots around town. I took taxis, too, when I had the extra dough. I could still walk to Clancy's, so that was good. Most of the time, Mom drove me to my weekly DUI classes. They sure did suck. At least they only went on for three months before I got my license back.

Other than the DUI, my lifestyle stayed the same. I still went to bars often; I just didn't drive myself there. Then—and I'm not proud of this—I started to dabble with cocaine and crystal meth sometimes. I just didn't care about anything. The fact was, I really didn't like myself, so anything that altered my reality was fine with me.

As I started using these drugs more often, I was determined to never become one of those users who did it every single day, or even weekly. Instead, I did it recreationally. The idea was that I'd have some good-ass times with plenty of downtime to recover. It took me more time to recover from crystal than from coke. I would guess that I was using those drugs about every other month—the cocaine maybe a little more. Because I'm naturally very thin, I lost five or six pounds each time I used meth. I figured I could never be a speed addict even if I wanted to, or else I'd melt away to nothing. I did have some fun times, just not when I was coming down. That part was horrendous. I'd need a few days of sleeping before I felt normal again. I never understood how someone could use all of the time.

One day, while I was alone at Clancy's, I played pool with a strange guy, and we got to talking. He knew I had a boyfriend, so it wasn't like that, but he told me he sold ecstasy. I'd done ecstasy once in high school, and I had a good experience with it. He said they were $20 a pop, but he would give me a freebie. I took the pill home with me, and that became the start of a new friendship with a new drug to use here and there. Naturally, since Lathan was just as much of a risk-taker as me, he also became involved.

I was using these drugs while my poor brain was still healing. I never had any worries about dying while using all these different drugs. Overdosing or having a bad reaction never crossed my mind, either. In my mind, I was unstoppable and immortal.

I really don't know who or what I was during this time in my life. I was living with zero purpose. Inside, I knew I still had some purpose that I was good for, but it felt inactive. Staying alive was good for my social life and my family. I think that was the only purpose I felt I had to offer then. I was always feeding the stray cats, so I was good for that, too—putting food in hungry tummies. But real, meaningful, productive feelings of purpose? I had none of those.

I do know there were a few things I felt strongly about. The first thing was that I wasn't in love with Lathan, and that our relationship would not last forever. There were many things about him I didn't like, and the longer we stayed together, the stronger I felt it. I hated the fact that he lived off me, and how much he lied. I also hated how he never wanted to cuddle. Every time I'd try, he'd say something like, "Get away, I feel too claustrophobic." I just knew it wasn't going to last, since I love to cuddle.

Another thing I knew about my future was that one day, I would give up smoking cigarettes. But the last thing I felt strongly about was the drug use. I understood that I was having such good times and that I wasn't concerned with anything important, but I also knew I didn't want to use these hardcore drugs forever. One day in the near future, I knew I would stop all of that madness. Something deep in my soul's core said that when I was truly ready to stop, I would. Just like that.

I wasn't ready yet, though. In the meantime, I was going to seriously live it up. We had lots of kick-backs at our apartment. After the bar closed, we'd invite our homies over and we'd all chill and party longer. Lots of times it would just be to smoke weed and have a few more beers. Other nights would get more intense. Our house was the go-to spot for people looking to get comfortably messed up.

CHAPTER 32

The Time Has Come

After having lived the same basic lifestyle for about two years, I could feel my mindset changing. Time was passing and things weren't as fun as they once were. I was really starting to get tired of Lathan. We had a weird relationship, and as it grew, our drug use increased. He also got worse about taking advantage of me. If I wasn't feeling well or simply didn't want to do anything, but he still wanted to go out to the bar, then he'd ask me for money. And I'd give it to him—usually like $20 or something. Then I'd stay home and chill alone, willingly enabling this behavior. I'll never deny that this whole situation was as much my fault as it was his. The partying had only gotten worse, and I stopped trusting him.

There were signs he was hooking up with another girl—one in particular, but there might have been others, too. This girl was such a shark; she even told me a few times that she thought my boyfriend was hot. She was this tweaker bitch that had attended Covina High School with me, and she was also a regular at Clancy's. She was a cute Asian girl that seemed to be a goody two-shoes in school, but she sure wasn't being good anymore. The difference between her meth use and mine was that she lived her life by the drug. She'd show up at Clancy's with another girl I went to high school with, who would also confirm that she wanted my man and that they were regular users. I felt like they'd hooked up already, but I didn't care that much. He was really starting to bother me. I was so close to being over him.

Then came the time my mom accused us of stealing her credit card and racking up a huge bill. I didn't know what she was talking about, but I somehow knew Lathan was to blame. We had been at their house a few times together, and I wouldn't put it past him to do something like that.

I didn't love him anymore. I don't think I ever really did. I cared for him, but that's all. He counted on me for everything, and I'd wanted that feeling of always having someone around. We did have things in common, had fun times together, and were attracted to one another, but the biggest part was that I held the key to the financial situation. He wouldn't willingly give that up.

He was a laid-back guy, but one night while we were both high on drugs we got into a huge fight. I ended up with a black eye, and I definitely gave him some bruises. I didn't like myself much before I met him. By then, I hated myself. I hated everything about me. I felt worthless. I felt the shittiest I'd ever felt. This wasn't a real and meaningful life I was living—quite the opposite. I was living in a screwed up, twisted reality. I absolutely hated being sober. It was the most boring and uncomfortable feeling ever. As long as I was able to get stoned, then I decided I didn't need anything else.

My overdue rent was piling up. I had just stopped paying it at some point. They never sent me a notice or anything about being late. This went on for several months. We didn't understand how they never contacted us and kept letting it ride. The only reason we could think of was that this apartment building was always under new management. It seemed like every other month there was a new manager. So maybe, somehow, we had slipped under the radar. Obviously, something like this would not last forever, but I was enjoying not having to pay rent for as long as I could.

I vividly remember a life-changing moment that occurred the night after another hardcore drug session. Standing in front of the bathroom mirror, I looked at my face, and then deep into my eyes. I looked absolutely horrible. My skin was pale, undernourished, dry, blotchy, and an unnatural, sickly color. I had dark bags under my eyes. I leaned in closer to stare even deeper; I looked long and hard. What looked back at me was pure sadness and disaster. A lonely, scared, dark, dismantled, lost soul. Flashbacks of my life danced threw my mind, but I had no idea who I was. The only thing I did know was that I didn't want to use bad drugs anymore. I knew things would only get worse if I continued to live this way. Looking deep into my soulful eyes, I said aloud, "I'm not going to use these hardcore drugs anymore."

I knew that night that the time had come.

I had come to the realization that it was now time for me to stop. I wasn't giving up weed or cigarettes yet, but it was a promise to myself that I would not use a bad drug again. I knew with all my heart, mind, body, spirit and soul. My mind was made up, and I would keep that promise from then on.

Meanwhile, Mom was worried about me. She didn't know about all the drugs I was using, but she knew Lathan was taking advantage of me and that I wasn't making smart choices. She knew about my hanging out in bars, my DUI, and my smoking pot. Maybe she assumed I sometimes used other drugs, too.

I knew something positive inside me was slowly taking place. It all started with that one night looking into the mirror. My maturity level was rising.

I told Lathan that he needed to find a job. I let him know how serious I was this time. He said he would try his hardest, like it was no big deal. Half of me believed him, but only half. I felt our relationship coming to an end, but I was still giving him one last chance to get it together.

For the next few weeks, I hounded him about finding a job. Finally, he told me he'd found some work at the Coca-Cola factory in Irwindale. It wasn't far from where we lived, and I was pleased to hear it. He would leave the apartment a couple of days a week to go to this job. He showed me a black work type shirt with his name tag on it. It all seemed totally legit.

But soon I started seeing inconsistencies in his story. I'd catch him in lies, and one day I found him at Clancy's when he was supposed to be at work. When I confronted him, he told me they let him go home early because there wasn't that much work for him to do that day. I felt he was lying to me, but couldn't figure out why. I let it slide, but knew in my heart that I needed to dig deeper.

So I called the factory one day and asked to speak to Lathan. He was supposed to be working that day, but they had never even heard of him. The guy I spoke to looked for his name in the system, then told me that nobody with that name worked there, or had ever worked there. I asked a few more questions to see if he could have been mistaken, but it was true. Lathan did not exist to them.

I got angry. I was fed up with his bullshit. It was nighttime, and I just knew he'd be at Clancy's. When I arrived at the bar to confront him, I asked someone outside to go in and get Lathan. He came out to the parking lot and I started yelling at him, calling him out. I told him all about the phone call I'd made earlier and who I spoke with. His first reaction was pure denial. He tried to keep reassuring me that he did work there, and that there must have been a mistake.

Finally, I told him if he didn't tell me the truth that it would be over between us. He saw how serious I was and came clean. The truth was that he never worked there. He'd been at someone's house or the bar when he said he was working. He told me how a friend got him the shirt and made a fake name tag. I was hurt, and even though I didn't tell him right then and there, our relationship was over. Later that week I told him how I felt.

He understood when I told him I was moving in with my mom and her new boyfriend, Ron. I had arranged for them to go on a date one night and they hit it off. As for Lathan, I wasn't feeling him anymore.

When I gave my notice to vacate the apartment, it had been five months since I'd paid any rent. I was so worried about the management figuring it out and charging me for all of it at once. All I could do was hope for the best. To my surprise, the amount they asked for before moving out made it seem as if their records indicated I'd been paying rent all along. How this happened, I'll never know.

Peaches, the cat we rescued at Mom's old condo, was going to stay behind. I felt awful—he'd lived with me for a while and I really loved him—but there were already too many cats coming with me and it wasn't my house. I had to say goodbye to all my outdoor kitty friends. I did feel bad that I wouldn't be able to give them food anymore, but this is the way it needed to be. I love you all. Goodbye. Goodbye, apartment. Goodbye, Lathan...for now.

CHAPTER 33

Lost Girl

Living with Mom and Ron in San Dimas (best known for the fun water park, Raging Waters, which Bill and Ted went to in their "excellent adventures") wasn't bad at all. They allowed my cats Halo, Rhino and Marley to live with them, too. Mom's cat and my old cat Jasmine was already there. They were indoor/outdoor pets at first, but they all became outdoor only cats at some point—all except for Halo and Rhino.

I finished my DUI program and continued to go to Clancy's. I still smoked pot and cigarettes daily, but avoided hardcore drugs.

There was an issue with my ex, though. Ever since we broke up, he no longer had a steady place to live. He was still unemployed, and, from what he told me, was staying at a few different friends' houses. I guess he was getting a little bit of money from his mom here and there. With that money, he'd eat fast food and occasionally be able to afford a motel. He was basically homeless.

I no longer loved him, but we did remain friends. We still talked a lot, and I felt bad for him. He would often still ask me for money, and I'd help him out when I could. I'd buy him a week at a nearby

Motel 6 or Super 8, and then there was the little bit of money I'd give him to eat as well. I could only afford so much.

Obviously, I couldn't make sure he had a motel every night. There were many nights he needed a place to sleep, and I told him he couldn't stay at my house. He knew that, and would figure it out on his own. One night he was desperate and asked if I could sneak him in and let him sleep under my bed. He climbed through my bedroom window when everyone else was fast asleep. Then, when Mom and Ron left for work in the morning, he left through the front door. It began to happen more often. On days when they didn't have to work, he'd sneak out the same way he came in.

Somehow, I felt he was my responsibility. I couldn't let him sleep outside in the cold, and on the nights he needed somewhere to sleep, he'd give me the heads-up about when he'd be coming over. It was usually after the bar closed or sometime late at night. He'd tap on my window a few times and I'd let him in. The window was small and high up off the ground, so it wasn't easy. I would always have some blankets and a pillow under my bed waiting for him. There was also a white bed skirt to protect him from being seen, just in case someone was to walk in. Once he was safely inside, we hardly talked. If we did, it was just a few quiet whispers before we fell asleep.

I will admit that many nights I got nervous and scared. I always knew there was a chance we would get caught, even though we were both extra careful. Everyone thought me and Lathan were totally over, so I would have been mortified if I'd been caught.

Since I didn't have a car, I took buses everywhere. I even took a bus to the bar lots of times. I had to take a taxi home after closing time, since buses didn't run that late. Even though I wasn't a big drinker, and never had been, I was a big pothead who loved playing pool and throwing darts. I became very good at both games. Believe it or not, I actually got called a pool shark. People who knew me knew my game and how well I played. Others that had just met me soon learned how good of a pool player I was. Once I learned how to hold a pool stick properly and understood how to see the shots and angles, slowly but surely, I became great. I had always been good at darts, but eventually I started to like pool more.

These games passed the time and made going to a bar so much fun. I'd only have one or two drinks, so I wasn't necessarily there for the alcohol. Besides, I felt obligated to get a drink if I went. I would have been perfectly content going there stoned and every two hours or so going out back to take a hit, but the type of bars they have in Amsterdam don't exist in California.

I guess it was nice having that one drink, as long as I could take my hit soon after. It wasn't nice to have a drink without it. I'd stay at the bar for about three hours on average. The same old heads were always there, and I always felt comfortable, never alone. When I went to bars other than Clancy's, I wouldn't stay as long. The people were different, but since all the bars were pretty much all around one another, I usually saw someone familiar. My second favorite bar was called Chatterbox. I didn't mind going to bars by myself. I could always hang out alone as long as I was playing my games. Either my quarters were up, or I was running the table for a little while. Going out alone was always an adventure, and I loved it.

I kept writing in my journals. Whenever I felt compelled to write something down, it always turned into a poem, whether I planned it that way or not. I guess poetry always came naturally to me. Having a pen and paper was always vital, as I was both deeply introverted and deeply extraverted. In both ways, I've always been able to vividly express my emotions. I've never been one to keep things inside. I always knew in my heart that writing was a big piece of my heart. It was an art form that I was always good at, passionate about.

Before I knew it, I was back on the road driving again. I made sure I never drove to a bar, or anywhere I might have a drink. About seven months later, I decided to drive myself to Elvie's. I knew I shouldn't, but I was in the area and thought I'd play a couple games of pool. I told myself that if I decided to have a drink, I'd call a taxi to go home. I had weed on me, so I didn't need a drink anyway.

I parked behind the bar and walked in through the back, recognizing a few faces. After the first game of pool, I decided to order myself a Red Bull and Grey Goose, light up a cigarette, and put more quarters down on the table. I started chatting it up with whoever was playing pool.

I drank and played my games. I went outside to smoke some weed from my little pipe and came back in. I was already planning on taking a taxi home, but I remembered being told that you can drink one shot, or one beer, and an hour later you'd be under the legal limit. Even if that were true, I shouldn't have thought about driving at all, not even five hours later. I started thinking that with my thin body, I'd be okay to drive after two hours. I'd play it extra safe, and I'd even save $20 on a taxi.

When the two-hour mark arrived, I was bored as hell and got into my car, so ready to get out of there. But something didn't feel right. I didn't feel tipsy or anything; it was something else. Going against my gut instinct, I drove away.

Halfway home, I couldn't help but be wary of the risk I was taking, and the fact that I'd had a drink a couple of hours earlier. I had a creepy, gross feeling in the pit of my stomach. The thought of getting pulled over weighed heavily on me, even though I didn't feel drunk or tipsy.

I came to a small intersection on Citrus Avenue and waited at the green light to safely make a left-hand turn. When the oncoming lane was clear, I made the turn just as the light was turning yellow. I wanted nothing more than to be safely at home. As I made that turn, I noticed a police car waiting for the light to turn green so he could go straight. For whatever reason, after I made my turn, he decided to switch lanes and turn right, following behind me.

At that point, my stomach dropped. It was a little after one in the morning, and I was the only car on the road. I was terrified. With the cop car trailing behind me, I had this feeling I would hear sirens soon. And I did. I was getting pulled over.

A thousand worries ran through my mind: my mom, handcuffs, another DUI, eighteen months of classes, and no car again. It was like a roller coaster of scary thoughts in my mind. I started hyperventilating as my car slowed down to a complete stop on the side of the road. Since I didn't feel tipsy, a part of me was confident that it would be okay. I'd never thought what I would do or say if I got pulled over again. After having a drink a couple of hours earlier, I never thought of not telling the truth. No one ever told me I could lie.

The officer came to my open window. He never told me why he stopped me, nor did I ask. The first thing he asked me was where was I coming from. I told him the truth. Then he asked me if I'd had anything to drink. I told the truth again. Right after I admitted that, the young officer told me to get out of the car. He asked me to walk in a straight line, which I did easily. Next, he had me recite the alphabet. I did that perfectly, too. Finally, he told me to say it backwards. I got a couple of letters wrong. I let him know I was sober. He knew I was good, too. Then I asked him how anyone could say the alphabet backwards without practicing. He said some people could.

Another police car pulled up behind him. This officer had a breathalyzer to check my blood alcohol level. He showed me what to do, then asked me to blow: 0.08.

He said that if it were up to him, he'd let me go. But it wasn't; it was up to his supervisor, who was on his way. I was told that normally I would have just been released, but the officer who was coming had lost a close family member to a drunk driver and was very hard on DUIs. Not good news to hear. And since this would be my second one, I was probably in even more trouble.

I was not feeling good about any of it. I didn't understand why these two cops couldn't make the decision. My mind and emotions were starting to go haywire by the time the third officer arrived. He was a much older man. The other cops told him my story first, then the older officer came over to talk to me. He told me that I shouldn't be drinking and driving, and that he was going to have to give me a DUI. I was crushed, devastated. I felt everything around me come tumbling down as he handcuffed me. On the ride to the station, he told me that my car wouldn't be towed and that I could go get it in the morning. One good thing, I guess.

After spending a night in jail, they released me at seven o'clock in the morning. They told me I had my license for one month before it would be taken from me. I walked twenty minutes from the police station to my car. There it was, waiting for me on Citrus Avenue and Hollenbeck Street. I couldn't believe this had happened—again. This dumb decision to go to the bar in my car and then try to drive home made me feel like the stupidest person in the world. I was doing so well not drinking and driving, too. Then I went and screwed it all up for one stupid, boring night out.

As I drove home, I started thinking ahead to eighteen months of classes, imagining how much community service I would have to do, and all the AA meetings I'd have to attend. I was told that I might have to do jail time. As dreadful as all that sounded, there was something that made me feel far more dreadful: having to tell my mom.

A week or so went by and I hadn't mentioned a word about the

DUI to anyone. I knew I would have to tell Mom before the month was up. I just didn't know when the right time would be. I felt so low. So crumby. So ashamed.

Mom's car was in the shop for some reason one day and she needed a ride home from work. Once she was sitting in my car and we were driving home, I promised myself I'd tell her.

I arrived at the delivery drop-off spot behind her work. My cute mom walked up to the car and I greeted her as we drove away. She started talking to me about something work-related. After she finished her story, I couldn't hold it in any longer. We drove through the mall parking lot, and I told her everything. She couldn't believe it. She looked and sounded so disappointed. Mom always tried to make the best out of every situation, but her face said a thousand words: all of them sad.

I'd broken her heart and trust yet again. Mom told me that I'd have to get a lawyer. My Uncle Van had an attorney friend who could help me, and a judge would soon determine my fate.

CHAPTER 34

Infatuated

I lost my license again, and for a whole lot longer this time. We retained the services of Uncle Van's lawyer friend in the hopes that he could lessen my sentence. The main thing we were trying to avoid was jail time.

My cat Rhino had gotten out of the San Dimas house and not returned. I felt awful and thought for sure he'd show up on our doorstep soon after, but sadly he never did.

Lathan still needed my help with money, motels, and sometimes a place to sleep. We went out together a few times, but strictly as friends. We'd take the bus together, meet up for lunches or coffee, and smoke cigarettes. At home, I continued to write my poetry, essays, and occasionally a song if a tune with lyrics flowed into my mind. When I didn't go out barhopping, I watched TV and listened to the radio in my room with Halo.

With the help of my lawyer, I was able to avoid jail time. Instead, I was sentenced to eighty hours of community service, twenty-six AA meetings, and eighteen months of DUI classes once a week for two hours each, along with a hefty court fine. After the first year of classes were complete, I'd be eligible to get a breathalyzer installed in my car so I could drive again for the last six months. This is what I got for frequenting the bar and being irresponsible while I did it.

Aside from attending my weekly DUI classes and doing the community service, I didn't have much else going for me. No job, no prospects. Annoyed and upset with my circumstances, I felt like I wasn't going anywhere in life. I knew, though, that I loved to write. I knew that my poetry was good. It was the one creative outlet I had that I could do well all by myself, and the only thing that truly made my heart, mind and soul feel good. Sure, it wasn't productive in the sense of me trying to sell it or make something of myself with it, but I always thought that maybe one day I could. That wasn't my focus, though. I wrote poetry because I loved to.

On Halloween night, 2008, I decided to take myself out to Clancy's for a drink and play a couple games of pool with whoever happened to be there. I didn't dress up, and the bar was pretty empty that night. I ordered a beer and started playing pool with some random guy. After a couple of games with this dude, I looked over at the bar and was surprised to find an incredibly hot guy sitting alone. There was something about him that made me want to go over and strike up a casual conversation.

My eyes were focused as I walked over to the bar and took the empty seat right next to this guy. I told the bartender to give me a Bud Light, trying to act as if I hadn't noticed the hot guy there yet. He was watching the television behind the bar and didn't look at me right away. Once I got my beer, I came out and asked him how he was enjoying his night.

He finally looked at me, smiled, and answered my question. I managed to keep the conversation flowing. His name was Fabio. We ended up talking for about twenty minutes before he told me he was waiting for two of his girl friends to get there. I felt a bit bummed, but got the impression he liked me.

When I got up to play another game of pool, I looked at him and he gave me this big, beautiful smile. While playing at the table, I glanced in his direction a few times and he was already staring at me. He wasn't smiling, but instead gave me these starry-eyed gazes, looking deep into my eyes from way across the room. Our eyes locked on each other for a good ten seconds each time. I could totally feel his passion, and I'm sure he could feel mine. This guy had me hypnotized. Butterflies danced in my stomach. Sweet seductive vibrations came over me. I'd never wanted someone more.

When the two girls he was waiting for finally arrived, they were actually two girls I knew. One was a bartender who worked there, and the other was her best friend. They were both cool enough, I guess. We'd chatted sometimes, but were never close. He mentioned he was a Navy Seal and had just gotten out of the service. He'd met these girls a few months earlier. Now that I knew who they were, I had all my confidence back.

I walked over there to tell the girls hi and mention how I'd met their friend earlier. Soon he started to ignore them; his attention was completely fixated on me. It was obvious he was putting them off. I could see their frustration and jealousy, but I didn't care. I loved that he was so into me.

Soon they got up to leave, having realized that they were getting his cold shoulder. We were glued to one another, and soon decided to leave the bar together.

I got in his car and we ended up going back to my house. It was late and everyone was sleeping. We sat in the living room and talked for a while. When he finally decided to get going, he asked for my phone number and I gladly gave it to him. I walked him outside, and he kissed me on my doorstep. I was infatuated with him from that moment on.

Over the next couple of days, I just daydreamed about him, praying and hoping he'd call. I would even listen to the song "Dreaming of You" by Selena on repeat as glorious visions of us together swam through my mind. Half of my heart worried he'd never call.

Later that week, while Lathan and I sat outside a coffee shop, my cell phone started vibrating. I looked down and saw a strange number with an area code matching where Fabio said he was staying. I got so giddy and excited inside, but I didn't want to show it in front of Lathan. I told him that I needed to take the call and stepped away.

When I answered the phone, Fabio casually asked what I was doing and I made up a story. I didn't want him to know I was out with another guy, let alone my ex-boyfriend. We talked for a few minutes and agreed to get together soon. I hung up and walked back over to sit with Lathan. Something inside me knew that my friendship with him and our little get-togethers wouldn't be going on much longer.

After Fabio and I went out, we became inseparable. He'd often stay over at my house, and some days I'd visit him at his coworker's house, where he was staying. They both worked in LA at some union job. They carpooled together, so their living situation worked out. The coworker smoked pot, so we'd have smoking sessions together whenever I stopped by.

I was putting Lathan off. I avoided his calls, and finally put my foot down about not being able to help him out anymore. I told him he would have to talk to his mom and find another way. I also told him about my new love interest. Eventually, our friendship ended.

I adored being in a new relationship. I was lost in a dream. My life was soon dedicated to Fabio. I thought I was so in love. Then again, it could have been extreme infatuation. I didn't know the difference. All I knew was that I was really feeling my new man.

After a few months of dating, seeing each other every night on weekdays and all day on weekends, he started talking about getting our own place together in LA so he could be closer to work. I was a hometown girl who'd lived close to my family my entire life, so it scared me a little. It wasn't that far away, but much further than anywhere I was used to. During busier commute times, traffic would make it hours away. But I was so into him that I would do anything to keep the relationship solid. Soon, the idea of moving to an unfamiliar place didn't seem that bad.

I looked online for places to rent at a reasonable price. He knew about the money I had; I told him. Obviously, I was still insecure and wanted him to know my worth, thinking it would make him want me even more. He had a good job in downtown LA, and we were planning on splitting the rent. Things were going to be different with him.

I found a little inexpensive studio apartment for rent in Highland Park. When we went there for the tour, the outside of the building was way more attractive than the inside. It was built in the 1940s and had an elegant, Victorian look to it. Either way, it was the best looking place in the area, and they accepted pets.

The inside of this place was definitely not appealing or modern at all. It was very small, but that wasn't the problem. The apartment was old, damp and creepy. I could tell that everything inside that studio, including the materials, appliances, and built-in table, were originally installed in 1946. The stove was the oldest and dirtiest I had ever seen. There were visible crumbs and dirt left behind by previous tenants. I wondered how anyone could really even clean a stove like that. Then there was the kitchen sink: deep, old, scratched, chipped, and with a smelly stench to it. We were told there was no garbage disposal. There never had been. I didn't like the sound of that. The built-in table in that tiny kitchen was made out of wood, engraved with scratches and graffiti, and had a metal pole holding it up.

The back door was old, loose, wobbly, weak and rusted. The lock worked, but there was no other security whatsoever. If someone really wanted to break in, all they'd have to do was give it one good, strong kick. There was one little window above the kitchen sink with a view of part of a tree. Apart from the cool black and white tiled kitchen floor, the place was ugly.

Fabio liked it, and we knew we wouldn't find anything cheaper, so we gave the lady our information. I still didn't want to fully commit; I was going to look around some more. I thought that even if I found a more expensive place, I could pay the difference. When we left, I told him how I really didn't like it, but somehow he convinced me it was the right choice and that everything was going to be okay. I trusted him, and I would've done anything for him as long as he was happy.

We ended up taking the place and found ourselves living in Highland Park. While he was at work, I had lots of time alone in that tiny, scary crib and neighborhood.

It was less scary when he was home with me, but every night we'd hear gunshots outside. Freaky to hear, but as long as we were inside, we didn't have anything to worry about. That flimsy back door with the cheap knob and lock was always on my mind, though.

There were two local weed shops nearby. One was much better: cheaper and classier than the other. While Fabio was away at work, I'd smoke, eat takeout food, and write poetry or whatever else I felt like writing. We didn't have a television. It was just me and my favorite, loving kitty cat Halo. I'd had many cats before, indoor and out, but there never was and never could be another cat like Halo. I never knew a cat could love so much. She had the gentlest soul. She meant everything to me. Having her around made life feel that much better. She made me feel so safe, loved and content.

Fabio had been working for about a month. One night during the workweek he decided to get really drunk. I never drank at home, only if I was out at a bar or something. I smoked weed and cigarettes, but that's all. When the morning arrived and it was time for him to get ready for work, he wouldn't get up, no matter how hard I tried to wake him. When he finally opened his eyes, he was barely coherent, and mumbled something about how he couldn't go to work and that he didn't feel good. I went back to sleep.

The next day, when he came home from work, he told me he'd been fired. I couldn't believe it. He had only missed one day. How could this be? I didn't know how to react, but I had a feeling that he'd quit and was lying to me. I didn't question him, though. I knew that until he found a new job, we were going to be spending a lot more time together. That didn't seem so bad, except for the fact that I would now be responsible for all the bills. I told myself it would only be for a little while; he'd get another job soon. Besides, it would be nice getting to spend quality time with my boyfriend.

Since Halo's best friend Rhino never came home, I felt she needed another cat buddy. Fabio also wanted to adopt a small dog. Halo had never been around dogs, but she had the sweetest personality in the world, so I figured she'd adapt just fine. At this point in my life, I felt I was ready and able to allow another dog into my heart. Fabio and I decided to go to a pet shop one day and we picked out a cute little calico kitty to bring home with us. I named her Kendall, after my favorite brand of wine at the time: Kendall Jackson. Later that week, while looking at different dogs for sale in the penny-saver magazine, I found a mixed terrier pug. I always told myself that if I ever decided to get another dog one day, it would be a pug. This wasn't a purebred pug, but something called him to me. So, we drove down to Compton one afternoon and picked up my new little boy. I'd planned to name him Zeus, but on the drive back home, my heart suddenly came up with a different name for him: Gangsta.

By this time, my year of DUI classes were up, and I was eligible to get a breathalyzer installed in my vehicle and drive again. I promised myself that I would never ever get another, DUI.

I never did.

CHAPTER 35

Dark Side

I started to see a side of Fabio that was anything but pleasant. It was a dark side that I definitely didn't like. He became mean, would put me down and call me bad names. He was condescending and tried to make me feel stupid and worthless, though deep in my heart I knew the awful things he told me weren't true.

I had already been through the craziest and worst shit—mentally and physically. I could feel the strong, positive changes in me. So I didn't take it to heart when he'd call me bad names like bitch, stupid, dumbass and more. I guess I allowed him to do it because I was so infatuated with him. I was submissive and not yet confident, and I still had those enabling ways.

He had to be right all of the time; that's how his mind worked. He told me once he was right ninety-nine percent of the time. He was dead serious. I couldn't believe a person like this actually existed. Whenever I argued back to let him know that he wasn't right about something, he wouldn't have it. "I'm not going to entertain you," he would say.

And as time went on, I only got firmer. I wouldn't just let him believe he was always right. I started to stand up for myself. Every time he'd say something that I disagreed with, I'd let him know. I'd tell him that it was impossible for someone to always be right. And then he'd brag about his bachelor's degree. My response to that was simply this: "You'd have to have a PhD in every subject known to man to think you could know everything. And even then, it wouldn't be possible!"

This handsome "Prince Charming" was driving me crazy.

One night we played hangman on a pad of paper with a pen. When one of our games was over and I'd won, he had a fit. He told me I'd written down letters he never said. His ego was a lot to handle. I always had to explain myself to him, to make him understand, but he never got it. I had to constantly fight for my point of view, and it was difficult to live with every single day. Meanwhile, I was paying for everything: his food, his beer, his cigarettes, his weed, his rent, his bills, his hygienic necessities, and so on. And the name-calling became ridiculous.

I was in the kitchen after another argument, and I decided to sit down at our scratched out kitchen table and write down every single name he called me on a regular basis. The list filled up an entire piece of legal paper. When I'd finished, I showed it to him. He looked at it for a couple of seconds and gave it right back to me.

The reason I wrote all these different names down was because every time I'd confronted him about it in the past, he'd always denied it. I felt that by listing them all, he couldn't deny it anymore. Every time one of those names came out of his mouth, I'd call him on it right then and there and show him that paper. It didn't matter, though, because in the end he didn't even have the decency to look at what I wrote down. I told him how much it hurt me, but he obviously didn't care. It was like living with someone in permanent denial. I entertained him by arguing back, but it was all so stupid and took so much hard work and energy on my part.

I was so tired, so frustrated, so lonely, and so sad. And I knew I didn't deserve this. No one deserved this kind of treatment. I suppose if I had kept enabling him, things might've been easier for me. I could have avoided a lot of strain on my mind and emotions by pretending it didn't bother me. But that would have been unhealthy, and, quite frankly, I didn't have it in me to deal with it anymore. At least the abuse was only verbal and emotional, not physical. Nonetheless, all abuse is depressing and toxic.

I later learned that there is a name for someone with this kind of temperament and behavior: narcissist. I knew right away this word fit my boyfriend like a glove. Narcissists rarely have the ability to feel compassion or empathy toward another, and have an exaggerated sense of self-importance. According to Webster's dictionary, Narcissism, Machiavellianism and Psychopathy go hand in hand. Some people may exhibit one, two or all three of these personality types. If one possesses all three, they combine to make up Narcissistic Personality Disorder. Fabio definitely had all three, and it's a pain in the ass to be around someone who is this sick and self-absorbed. People who put up with such disgusting personalities are enablers to some degree. I was an enabler, but I couldn't stand being one any longer.

I was tired of this guy. I disliked him and how he would talk about his desire to move to another country and start a family. I would tell him no, that if I ever started a family of my own, I'd want my existing family to be a part of our lives. He'd go on to say how that's not the way it should be, and that I should leave my family behind and start a new one with him somewhere else. I knew I'd never allow it. The sound of all these plans made me sick to my stomach. If there was ever a time to trust my gut instinct, it was then.

I'd wonder if he'd hurt me badly if I moved away with him, or if he'd kill me one day if he got me somewhere far away. I didn't really know much about intuition back then, but mine was telling me to get as far away from him as possible. I felt that if I stayed with this guy, I would have to say goodbye to Rosemary—and she was just starting to really come back to me. I would never be happy; in fact, I'd probably be scared for the rest of my life. I knew in my heart of hearts that this guy was terribly wrong for me. His soul was dark, he was cold, he was mean, and he was starting to truly frighten me.

While we were together, I never told my family much about our lives. There were little bits and pieces that I would share with them. I shared more information with my sister Destiny. When I told Destiny about his plans for our future and that he wanted to move far away and start that family while I left my old one behind, she told me that if I stayed with him and moved away, he would kill me. She said she felt it. I agreed with her since I felt it, too.

My mom and sisters slowly started to realize he was a wolf in sheep's clothing. I always knew that and eventually told him so. He always talked negative shit about my beautiful, adoring family: another prime example of why Fabio was bad news. I would stick up for them every time. He'd run his mouth, but I never believed the stuff he said. For the sake of keeping the peace, lots of times I'd let it go in one ear and out the other. He would say nasty things about my mother, my grandmother, my sisters, and even my first little niece Azalea, who was barely a year old. But he knew nothing about my family history, and often made wrong and intentionally mean assumptions. Although I didn't believe what he said, it was hurtful to hear someone talk badly about the people I love.

I knew this wasn't going to last much longer. I asked him a few times about getting some help, and even offered to pay for it. I thought he might've had PTSD or Narcissistic personality disorder, and could get some help. Even after all his craziness, I was still willing to give him the benefit of the doubt. He didn't want help, and insisted there was nothing wrong with him.

Whenever I came home from visiting my family, Fabio would say how much he hated when I'd hang around my sisters. He'd go on about how they were so fake, how he hated the way they acted, and how every time I came home from seeing them, I acted just like them. He was a scumbag and I'd argue with him, but I was still with him. Dealing with him made me so much stronger on every level, having to fight for my rights every single day validated how much better I was, and how far I had come. I wouldn't have been able to stand up to him with my injured brain. I had become a fighter, which, come to think of it, I'd always been—in one way or another. When he told me I was stupid, I'd remind myself, "Hey, I know what it's like to really feel stupid, to not be in my right mind and to be unable to do anything about it except wait for my brain to heal. I'm not stupid anymore. I'm not incoherent anymore. I'm not that poor, helpless, unfortunate soul anymore. I am well now. I can talk freely, and I know exactly what I'm talking about!"

My brain and mind had healed immensely. I could think clearly. I could focus. I was strong. I was smart. I was able. I would no longer allow somebody to make me feel so awful when I knew what it was like to feel that way without anybody even having to tell me. I knew how far I'd come.

I had waited almost a decade for Rosemary to return. I was ready to move back to my hometown and be near my family, where I felt far more comfortable. There was no longer any reason for me to be living out there in that gross apartment with that self-absorbed man on that scary street in Highland Park.

I was the financially secure one. I could make all my own choices now. When I let him know that I was going to find a place back home and leave my notice as soon as possible, he got mad. But I didn't care what he wanted anymore. He had only fueled my fire.

When I found a place in Pomona, on the border of the city of La Verne, I knew that it was where I wanted to be. My family would be close by again, just two cities away.

Even though I knew that I didn't want to be with Fabio anymore, I still let him stay with me for a little while at my new apartment. It was in a complex called Villa del Sol. He had nowhere else to go, and basically followed me there. He had seen the change in me and knew the way I felt; we had already talked about breaking up.

As tired as I was of his bullshit, and how surely things between us were deteriorating, he still couldn't help but be who he was. I kept putting my foot down, letting him know that all the crap wouldn't be tolerated if he stayed. He acted like he understood, but after a couple of days, I guess he just couldn't help himself. I dealt with it for about a month until enough was finally enough and I told him to get the hell out!

He had family that lived in Colorado; he talked about being closest with his dad and one of his brothers. He also said good things about his only sister. On the other hand, he wasn't close at all to his mom and other two brothers. He only said bad things about them. It wasn't my problem—he needed to go, and he knew it. I finally forced him to call them.

It was a sunny day. Fabio called his brother and told him how he needed an emergency plane ticket home. He packed his bags and left the next morning. I never saw him again. We talked on the phone a few times, and he wanted me to fly out to Colorado to meet his family. I actually thought about it, though I don't know why. In the end, I decided not to go. Our last phone conversation didn't go well, and from that day on, we never spoke again.

CHAPTER 36

Rosemary Reunites with Rosemary

It was November 2009. It was just me, my dog Gangsta, and my two cats, Halo and Kendall. I felt so strong and free. The time had come where me and the old Rosemary could finally meet again and rekindle our relationship. She was back, and better than ever.

It felt great, as though I'd lived many lives in one. My heart and head no longer ached. I'd survived. I'd conquered. I'd surpassed expectations in so many ways when I thought I couldn't, but I'd always kept hope, faith, and deep love in my heart. This was how it was meant to be. Everything suddenly made sense.

Rosemary went through so much suffering and pain. She was held captive for many years by her healing brain. At one time, she was insane, crazy, and couldn't comprehend even the smallest of things. Nothing made sense, and there were times she wanted to quit, give up, even die. But now the storm was finally over.

Something had drastically changed inside me. I felt reborn on so many levels, and I was getting to know myself all over again: the young me, the older me, and the new me as well. Putting it all into perspective, I figured I was now the new Rosemary, or even the new and improved Rosemary.

I lovingly embraced all of those long lost precious parts of myself. After having been disconnected for so long, that new phase felt amazing and transformative. I would say that was my thirtieth stage of recovery. From that moment on, I promised myself to only continue to get better and better with each passing day, and to grow, learn, love and experience life in a spectacular new way.

I started writing poetry every day—sometimes only one, and other times as many as five poems. I would write whenever and wherever my heart desired, and I had so much newfound inspiration. Whenever it happened, I'd grab one of my many journals and write away. It felt so good to express all of the words and pure poetry inside of me. I wrote until my heart was content, and the poetry flew out onto the page naturally. I never had to work at it or think much about it. It was all driven by raw emotion. For the first time since my car accident, a beautiful melody with matching words rushed through me. I was inspired to write a lovely new song.

"Wonder"

Late at night, all alone

Then I sit and I wonder
Where I've been, how I've grown
And how I've just been so under

And then I think and I wonder again
Was it really just fate and
Who's really my friend

And I wonder . . .

ROSEMARY REUNITES WITH ROSEMARY

After that, so many more songs flowed through me whenever they wanted. I felt like an open vessel.

There were many times both before and after my accident in which I took my life for granted. I had committed many wrongful acts. I couldn't and didn't see the light for some time. I needed to be pushed down to wake back up.

Nobody knew this new Rosemary yet. My family, my old friends and acquaintances, anyone who had ever known me—none of them would ever dream I could be this way. Even my family, who knew me better than anyone, didn't know exactly what I'd been through, what it felt like, and of course, what I'd become. I felt so wonderful, alive and well, and I was only months away from that decade milestone.

I don't regret anyone or anything that has happened to me in my past. It's all made me realize what I do and don't want in my future experiences. I've learned, I've grown, I've evolved, and I am only stronger and wiser for it. I'll continue learning, growing and healing every day. I've learned lessons the hard way, but now I'll only be going forward.

My family saw me about once a week, sometimes more and sometimes less, since I'd been living on my own. I wanted that feeling of truly belonging in this world again. For the first time in what seems like forever, I could feel myself truly blossoming.

I knew this in my heart and mind, but no one else did yet. I had a lot to prove. I had to show my family how much I'd matured, how much I'd grown, how much my brain had healed, how wise I'd become through my experiences, and what a strong, kind, loving, empathetic girl I was. I couldn't wait for the day where I'd truly feel a part of my family again.

I really took to heart everything my neurologist had told me years ago. He said I'd come back, and that I would heal. He said in ten to twelve years I'd know what I was left with. Also, that my brain would continue to heal for the rest of my life. It hadn't been quite ten years, but I was back, and I knew it. I felt like the happiest and most grateful girl in the entire universe.

Feeling like Rosemary again, after all those years was almost indescribable. To be reunited with her was pure magic and music to my soul.

CHAPTER 37

Just Me and My Animals

Getting that new apartment for just me and my animals felt amazing. It was a big upstairs apartment with two bedrooms, a huge living room and kitchen, and one decent sized bathroom. It also had a big balcony with a gorgeous view. There was a big palm tree hovering around it; I could even touch it if I wanted to. One big branch literally dangled over one side of the balcony: a perfect place to relax, write and dream.

Learning about myself and all I'd become was going to be a perfect new chapter. I adopted another cat and named her Ginger. I also ended up taking care of Mom's cat Jasmine for a while. Then there was my Halo, Kendall and Gangsta. As of Christmas, 2009, I had four cats and a dog living with me, and couldn't be happier.

Life without a boyfriend was different. I remembered the good parts of having one as well as the bad. I knew I was going to enjoy being single, being able to breathe and think for myself again, and so much more—it was all pure, relaxing music to my ears. Learning to fall in love with myself for the first time in almost a decade felt spectacular.

One afternoon, a friend and I went to Venice Beach and I got my first license to buy marijuana. I was still smoking pot every day to feel normal, but now I could buy it legally. I hadn't slowed down on that yet. I didn't even get that true high anymore. I never thought I would ever want to stop completely, but I did want to slow down a bit so I could actually feel high again. Slowly but surely, I started to smoke only at night. That meant I had more energy during the days to get stuff accomplished. Coffee by day, weed by night. That new regimen worked out beautifully.

I took myself out to a local bar once or twice a week to shoot some pool and play darts. I always loved those two games, and needed to get out and be around people sometimes.

I saw my family often. We always had each other's backs. Having tight bonds with my mom, my grandma, and my sisters was like having all the gold in the world.

My sister Alyssa and her longtime boyfriend, Jaromir (who I just so happened to introduce her to) ended up having a little baby girl; they named her Azalea. I was an aunt for the first time, and it felt amazing. A year and a half later, my sister Destiny had a little boy. His name became, Ethan. It was a wonderful new beginning for all of us, and things only got better. Soon after that, my brother married and they had a little girl and then a boy: Kourtney and Will. I didn't think I'd ever have kids, besides my animals, but that was totally okay. I loved being a fun, cool and awesome auntie.

Times were definitely changing, and I got to the point in my life where I was finally ready to give up smoking cigarettes. On August 6, 2010, I quit cold turkey.

CHAPTER 38

Beyond Empathetic

There came a time when I was able to assess my life through a different lens.

If there comes a time in your life when you can honestly look back on who and what you've been so far, take the opportunity. Don't ignore it. You'll find some decisions you made stupid, embarrassing and unlawful, but that's okay. You'll also find happy, fun and joyful memories. Everyone has some of each. If you look past where you've been and bring yourself to this very moment, you'll realize, that's all that matters: where you are right now. And if you think about regrets and things you could have done differently, bring your focus right back to the now and think about all the things you've done right. You've lived through it all and have made it this far. We live, we learn, we grow, we change; that's the process of life. So, since change is inevitable, why not change for the better? We always have a choice.

The craziest observation thus far is that the father of my first-born niece Azalea happens to be the brother of that guy I fell for at the Long Beach party I went to the night I stole my grandma's car. Skyler thought that maybe they'd like one another, so one night we all got together, and it turned out his hunch was correct. If I hadn't stolen my grandma's car, Azalea probably wouldn't have come into our lives. Strange how one of my biggest regrets would later give me one of my greatest treasures. Life sure is interesting, and to every negative there is a positive—if you dare to look for it.

Once I felt my mental wellness evening out, I realized there was something else that was distracting and disturbing me. I didn't worry about myself anymore, and I became extra sensitive to all life forms: human beings, animals, insects, and even trees and flowers. I started to pick up on all their energies without even trying. Soon, I couldn't even watch the news without crying my eyes out. If I went to a store, a street fair, or anywhere with lots of people around, I could feel all of their energies to the point that it became overwhelming and I'd start to feel dizzy and faint.

While walking my dog, I was always mindful of my surroundings. I'd notice beautiful things along with everything that wasn't so beautiful. If a tree or a plant was dying, I'd feel pricks in my heart or a sick feeling in my stomach. If there were snails or roly polies on the sidewalk, and if either of us accidentally stepped on one, I'd feel horrible. I'd try to see if there was a way to save their lives. If not, I felt their poor little lives slipping away. I'd see bees dying, and I'd burst out crying as I felt their suffering. If there was a skinny, hungry, homeless cat, I'd have to feed it right away. If that wasn't possible, I'd cry again and feel miserable; the rest of my day would be ruined. Witnessing suffering firsthand is what affected me the most. I seemed to have no control over these feelings and sudden reactions. I didn't know what was happening to me or why I felt this way. I couldn't control myself, and it felt like I was going crazy again, but this time in a totally different way. I needed to get help and figure out what the heck was going on with me.

I eventually saw a therapist, who told me that I was an empath. He also said that lots of other doctors wouldn't tell me that or agree with him, but he knew this type of behavior very well. Someone who is simply empathetic toward another feels an emotion that can arise from time to time in certain conditions and under particular circumstances. An actual empath, on the other hand, feels the pains of others constantly and consistently. They are always affected by everyone and everything all of the time, and it affects their overall well-being.

After he and I spoke, I understood and knew this empath person he was describing was me to a tee, but I also knew I couldn't go on living like this forever; I'd die of sadness. I needed to gain control over these feelings and abilities. That night, I stayed up late researching all I could about empaths. I lived with these hardcore emotions taking over my life for a good three years, until one day, I embarked on a truly life-changing journey of discovery.

CHAPTER 39

Learning and Evolving

Everything that I had been through only made me want to learn as much as I could about the human mind and its spiritual, emotional and physical connections. I had come so far through faith and love and never giving up. I didn't know any better then, but now I was determined that I would. I always believed that somehow, some way, things would get better. I had so much more life to live, and knew that things would work out as long as I kept searching and believing. I didn't know how, but I knew it was possible with a positive outlook and unwavering faith.

As wonderful as it is to care, love and help people in all possible ways, I knew that I needed to get this empath thing under control. How could I help anyone if I felt so miserable, small and helpless all the time? I prayed to the universe for answers. I tried to not put a time limit on things and went with the flow.

I had the idea of writing this book back in 2009, and wrote an outline while I was still at the Highland Park apartment, but something inside me said that I had a lot more living to do. I accepted that, and in 2014, I felt inspiration coming through here and there and started writing again. But skepticism distracted me. It didn't feel good at all. After trying many techniques like mindfulness, deliberate appreciation, praying, living in the here and now, and saying positive affirmations daily, something amazing happened.

I was walking through a local Barnes & Noble, and as I browsed through the different books in the inspirational section, I noticed one sticking out so far off the shelf that it seemed like it was about to fall. I grabbed it. It was beautifully designed with pretty gold lettering. It was *The Artist's Way* by Julia Cameron. The beauty of the book mesmerized me, as well as the energy I felt while holding it. Something about it felt extra special. It put a smile on my face. I trusted my intuition and bought it. It was a self-help book, but it felt like so much more and I was excited to bring this magical book home.

The next day, I got to working with it. After I completed the eight-week program, my overall knowledge and happiness improved by a good ninety percent. It gave me the confidence and guidance to finish writing this book. I am very thankful.

From then on, I taught myself more and more about the human and spiritual realm. None of it was religious, but all of it was spiritual. In fact, it was spiritual mixed with science, but to be honest with you, I don't think that science can explain a lot of it because it hasn't evolved that much yet. Each individual must prove their own universally given powers to themselves. Nonetheless, science has made giant strides in the mind-body connection area. I spent hours each day learning all I could about energy, vibrations, frequencies, how all of those things are what we're made of, and how the mind and body mirror each other and relates to everything that happens in our physical experience. Just as we create things we don't want with our vibrations, with a little practice we can learn to create the things we do want, and so much more.

All emotions we experience vibrate at different frequencies. Negative emotions like depression, sadness and fear vibrate at the lowest frequencies, and positive ones like love, joy and appreciation vibrate at the highest. Anger vibrates a little higher than sadness, and hope higher than anger. I've come to understand that this is true in the physical, spiritual and scientific realms if you truly study all aspects of them together. The most interesting thing about all of this is that once I started to learn, understand, and practice ways to vibrate on a higher level daily, life suddenly looked different and changed drastically for the better—both around and within me. Everything started to resonate with my whole being. I delved into this headfirst, and kept digging deeper and deeper. The better I got at controlling my mind, thoughts and emotions, the more wellness, health, synchronicities, and other great things I experienced.

I started practicing meditation for about twenty minutes a day until I got really good at it. That alone was life-changing. One doesn't need more than that each day to show drastic improvements in all areas of their lives. I trained myself to focus on the good in life and what I want, rather than focusing on the bad and what I don't want. I also noticed that the fastest ways to increase your vibration is through appreciation, meditation, writing down positive aspects of your life, and watching a program that makes you laugh and feel good. Laughter really is one of the best medicines. Visualization is also a great high vibrational tool.

Everyone who has practiced and applied these knowledgeable things to their lives like I have will tell you the same. So many incredible stories told by people all around the world, will likely mention something about the powerful mind-body connection. It takes desire, belief, expectation, application, and knowing that you'll be a survivor, too.

The body is a brilliant mechanism with trillions of cells, and everything I mentioned, when practiced and incorporated into a person's life, can help make a sick person well and a healthy person live optimally. It takes belief and consistency when it comes to taking care of your energy field. Anyone can learn this stuff, if feeling happier and healthier is a priority for you. Go ahead and prove it to yourself. Slow and steady really does win the race.

It only takes a few weeks of dedication and practice to master these techniques. And there are others too, but these are just the one's I use. It might feel hard in the beginning, but it will make all the difference in the long run. I'd say the most positive changes I've noticed in my life are in my health, happiness levels, improved looks, and my overall quality of life. For example, I once had fibromyalgia quite badly, and I have cured myself of that. With some or all of these practices, one can cure themselves of unwanted things they are experiencing. If you look up "Epigenetics," you'll see how far science has proved this to be true. Still, I can't wait until science really starts studying frequencies more and how they relate to the mind-body connection. It's time they start measuring the frequencies of our thoughts, emotions, and so much more. Humans need to know just how much power our minds, emotions and thoughts hold over how we experience our reality. Life would be so much better for everyone if they decided to take the initiative on this crucial next step in human evolution and expand on the great Albert Einstein's theory that, "Future medicine will be the medicine of frequencies." It's time.

I feel better today than I have ever felt in my entire life, and it's thanks to my life experience, dedication, and desire to learn and practice as much as I can about our existence here on planet Earth. According to the psychology books, it takes twenty-one days of implementing a new ritual before it becomes habitual. I've found that to be true.

Controlling the mind and one's vibrational stance is key to everything we desire in life. Love and like vibrations are the most powerful forces in this entire universe, and I've come to learn that the universe doesn't choose favorites; it simply responds to vibrations. This knowledge has changed me forever, and I want to share all that I've learned with as many people as possible so that they, too, can become the healthiest and best versions of themselves, overcome challenges, and learn to live their lives to the fullest.

I also would like to mention how having animals by my side has made my life so much happier and more peaceful. Today, I have my dog Gangsta, who is ten years old, and my two gorgeous kitty cats Barnaby and Evander, who are four years old and brothers. I have a boyfriend that I've been with for years; he is a great guy, supportive, encouraging, and loving.

It was a long, rocky and very bumpy road for me, but with consistency and dedication to improving myself wholeheartedly, I can honestly say that, as of 2018, I have been living my best life possible. I also learned to not get mad at myself when I feel negative emotions, knowing that it's a normal thing for human beings to experience contrast sometimes. It's all a part of the process. The important thing is to just make sure I don't stay there long, so that I don't build up negative momentum. That's the challenge, but it becomes easier the more you practice. At last, life makes amazing sense.

Scientists and doctors have done wonderful things. People can live with conditions that would have killed them a few years ago. And that's wonderful! But, there's another process that the medical community is slowly catching onto: the medicinal healing power of our own minds.

A good way of understanding it is viewing medicine in the context of energy. We need to see energy in the context of vibration. We need to see vibration in the context of emotion. Then, we need to see emotion, not as feeling down when something happens that we don't like, but in the context of, "I want to feel a little better," followed by, "I want to feel a little better." It's important that we practice this thought process despite anything life throws at us. When we distract ourselves from the problem, the body stops resisting it, and allows natural healing to take place. If we follow this method, we stop doing the thing that prevents our natural healing processes from taking place. This is self-healing.

It's all about momentum. Every single day we add to the momentum of something, wanted or unwanted. Once we consciously choose to focus on things that make us feel better, we train ourselves to think positively, and things simply improve from there. We are all energy; even our thoughts are energy, and like energy attracts like energy. Anyone who puts in the energy work will prove to themselves that it isn't words that teach us, but life experience. They say that time is a great healer, but what really heals someone is the energy we put in as time passes. Wayne Dyer said it perfectly when he said, "You'll see it when you believe it."

CHAPTER 40

The Magnetic Pull

In 2018, I had a strong desire to travel to another country. I had never been abroad before, and something inside me wanted it more than ever. Whether someone was going to travel with me or not, I would soon be on my way to somewhere new. It felt like a calling from my soul.

I continued to follow my heart and trust my intuition. Lots of different places around the world looked intriguing, but somewhere in Europe was my first choice because I'd wanted to travel there ever since I was a little girl.

One day, while on social media, I came across a video. In it, a group of six people would get together once or twice a year and visit a particular country. I looked up the business and saw that it was legitimate. I would be traveling with like-minded people who also wanted to better their lives and explore another country. Gran Canaria, one of Spain's Canary Islands, was the destination. I knew this was the opportunity my soul was waiting for.

I applied and it was soon confirmed that I would be going to Spain with five other people. My boyfriend and family worried about me going, and I listened to and understood their concerns, but knew it was something I had to do for my well-being. I knew myself more deeply and profoundly than ever before, and this was something I'd thought out, and that I had to do for my evolution. I knew in my heart and gut that this was right; I'd never been surer about something in my life. It was all going to work out perfectly.

A magnetic pull and a soul calling are the best ways to describe those deep feelings. I was going and nobody could stop me.

And I did it! I had an amazing time with my group. It was so much fun, an incredible, eye-opening, beautiful and platonic experience. It was perfectly orchestrated, just as my intuition knew it would be. We all shared our life stories, plus lots of laughter and learning, all while discovering a magnificent place surrounded by pure, positive energy.

The experience only made me stronger. I also climbed a mountain for a total of about five hours with my tribe. It was unexpected and daring, but I did it. When I had to swing across a zip line in order to travel back down the mountain, two of my fellow travelers videoed me doing it. That's cool footage to have today, and I never told anyone until I arrived back home. I didn't want to worry them, and besides—I needed extreme positive focus that day. I grew braver just by doing that. It's safe to say that I don't think I will ever climb another mountain for the rest of my life, though—at least not one that big!

I came home feeling more alive, powerful and evolved. The people were great and I made long lasting friendships. I was so proud of myself. As I took a minute to reflect on where I'd been, how far I'd come, and where I was headed in life, I felt like the richest girl in the world.

When 2019 came around, I ended up traveling to two more countries. The second trip was to Banff, Canada, and the third was to London, England. So, within a year I had been to three new countries.

The memory comes back to me once more as I look back on everywhere I've been, everything I've done, and all the different emotions I've felt. That innocent teenaged Rosemary standing in the fast lane of the Corona Freeway, watching the speeding car approach from a distance. The sun setting. I slowly sit down in my car seat and take a breath, bracing myself as the car looms closer in my rear-view mirror. I close my eyes.

"Wow, Rosemary. It's been a long time since that tragic, yet fortunate day. We sure have come a long way, haven't we? Thanks for coming back to me, and for staying with me this time. I have a lot to live for and experience from this day forward. You are me, the real me. I love you."

"My Wonderland"

As I look deep into my soul
I see all the wounds I've had to sew,
From broken hearts to broken bones,
From feeling deathly and all alone.

For many years
I've lived only to survive,
Thanking my lucky stars, I had a family
To make me feel somewhat alive.

Sands of time
Winds of change
Living, growing,
Life slowly getting rearranged.

What got me by during the worst times of my life
Was the idea of the Rosemary,
Whom God The Universe
Had survived.

I'd been given many second chances
But there is one fact that is clear,
Holding the vision of my future self
So strong, so healthy, with the absence of fears.

I held that vision a long time ago,
Knowing that it wasn't real then
But what kept me going,
Was the feeling that she'd fully come back to me again.

SAN GABRIEL VALLEY GIRL

Rosemary,
That's me!
Unless you know my past,
You only see what the naked eye wants you to see.

Today I sit here and often stand
As a grateful, loving and honored girl
In a bright new World,
I call Wonderland.

I fought, I embraced, I endured the unthinkable.
With power in my heart, belief in my soul,
And a deep sense of intending to overcome it all,
It has led me to today,
A woman, who is so powerful, loving and strong.

Although I had imagined
To one day be and feel this way,
I've far exceeded my expectations
Living my life purpose now,
With so much appreciation, majesty and grace.

I know we've all had to fight one way or another,
Or else we wouldn't be living in this thing,
Called life.

What I am destined to say here today
Is that no matter what you are going through,
There is an option, a choice, a way.

To believe, have faith and envision
Your happiest and healthiest self.
Make peace with your present,
Make peace with your past,
Be as optimistic as you can
With today and your future,
Never give up hope,
Truly know and please feel in your heart that,
YES
This too shall pass.

What does an author stand to gain by asking for reader feedback? A lot. In fact, what we can gain is so important in the publishing world, that they've coined a catchy name for it.

It's called "social proof." And in this age of social media sharing, without social proof, an author may as well be invisible.

So if you've enjoyed *San Gabriel Valley Girl*, please consider giving it some visibility by reviewing it on Amazon or Goodreads. A review doesn't have to be a long critical essay. Just a few words expressing your thoughts, which could help potential readers decide whether they would enjoy it, too.

www.ingramcontent.com/pod-product-compliance
Lightning Source LLC
Chambersburg PA
CBHW030319100526
44592CB00010B/493